# Contents

# Selected Composer Biographies

**Fernando Carulli** was born in Naples, Italy, on February 10, 1770, the son of a famous statesman. Carulli's first musical instruction was on 'cello; however, he was soon attracted to the guitar. Carulli was entirely self taught as a guitarist, yet he rapidly became known as one of the leading virtuosi of his day. In 1808 he moved to Paris, where he was to make his home for the rest of his life. He was an extremely prolific composer, writing a great number of solos as well as chamber works for the guitar. Carulli died in Paris on February 17, 1841.

❖

**Fernando Sor** is considered to be the most important nineteenth-century composer of works for the guitar. He was born in Barcelona, Spain on February 2, 1778, the son of a well-to-do Catalan merchant. Sor received his first musical instruction at the monastery of Montserrat. At eighteen, he composed his first opera, *Telemachus on Calypso's Isle*, which was performed in Barcelona in 1797 to tremendous acclaim. In 1812, Sor moved to Paris and established himself as a great guitar virtuoso and composer. It was around this time that the music critic Fétis dubbed him "the Beethoven of the guitar." He made his London début in 1815 to great acclaim, and, in 1820, he moved to Russia where he produced three ballets. In 1830, Sor published his famous *Method pour la Guitar*, one of the finest methods ever written. He died in Paris on July 10, 1839.

❖

**Joseph Küffner** born in 1776, was a contemporary of Beethoven. He played violin with the court orchestra in his home city of Würzburg and later rose to become bandmaster in the Bavarian Army. Küffner composed seven symphonies and many works for chamber music ensembles. He also wrote a number of pieces for classical guitar, several of which are included here.

# Fifty Great Pieces for

# Easy Classical Guitar

Arranged and edited by **Jerry Willard**.

Music arranged by Jerry Willard.
Edited by David Bradley.
CD recorded by Jerry Willard.
Project editor: Adrian Hopkins.

CD mixed and mastered by Jonas Persson.

Order No. AM1005939
ISBN: 978-1-78038-854-0

Exclusive Distributors:
**Hal Leonard**
7777 West Bluemound Road
Milwaukee, WI 53213
Email: info@halleonard.com

**Hal Leonard Europe Limited**
42 Wigmore Street
Marylebone, London, W1U 2RY
Email: info@halleonardeurope.com

**Hal Leonard Australia Pty. Ltd.**
4 Lentara Court
Cheltenham, Victoria, 3192 Australia
Email: info@halleonard.com.au

**Jacques Bosch** also known as Jaime Felipe José Bosch, was a Catalan
guitarist and song writer born in Barcelona in 1825. He made his reputation
(and acquired a Gallic first name) in Paris where he became a popular teacher
of the guitar.

❖

**Adrian Le Roy** was born in 1520 to a wealthy family in the French town of
Montreuil-sur-Mer. Le Roy and his cousin Robert Ballard founded the printing
firm Le Roy & Ballard and in August 1551 obtained a royal privilege from
Henry II to print music. From the 1570s onwards this company enjoyed a
virtual music publishing monopoly after rivals dropped out of the market.
Le Roy himself would publish at least five volumes of lute and guitar music as
well as music by the composer Orlando de Lassus.

❖

**Johann Mertz** was born in Hungary and was to find success as a
virtuoso guitarist touring Russia, Moravia and Poland. Mertz's guitar music,
unlike that of most of his contemporaries, followed the pianistic models of
Chopin, Mendelssohn, Schubert and Schumann, rather than the classical
models of Mozart and Haydn or the *bel canto* style of Rossini.

❖

**Niccolo Paganini** was born in Genoa in 1782. Having first learned to
play the mandolin from his father, he moved on to violin at the age of seven.
Paganini was to achieve great success performing all over Europe and his
Caprice No. 24 in A minor is still considered by performers to be one of
the most difficult violin pieces ever composed. Most of Paganini's 100 or
so compositions were for violin, but he also wrote several pieces for guitar.

# Andantino

Joseph Kuffner (1776–1856)

# Poco allegretto

Ferdinando Carulli (1770–1841)

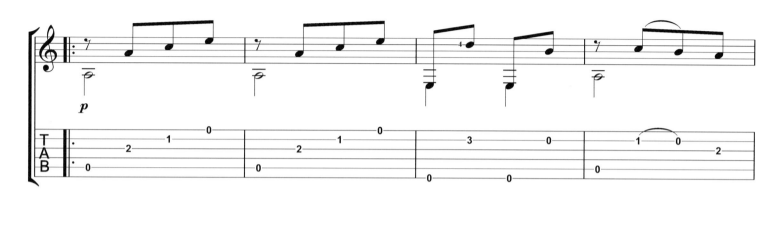

*D.C. al Fine*

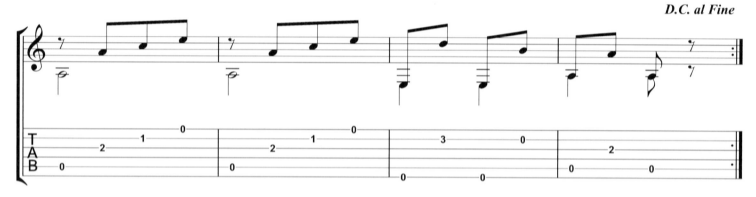

# Sonatina

Ferdinando Carulli

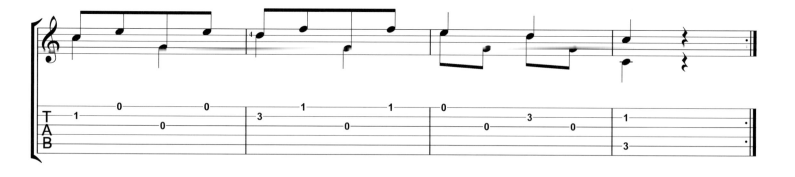

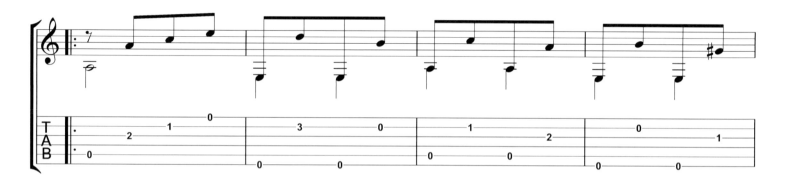

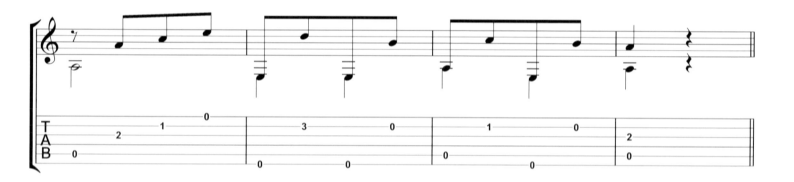

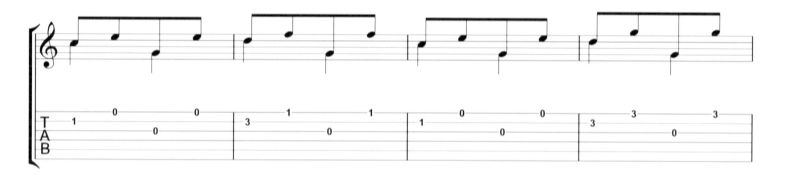

# Andante

Ferdinando Carulli

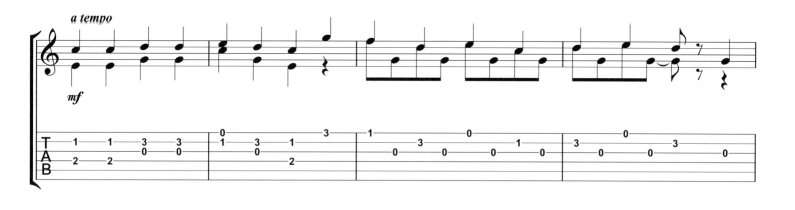

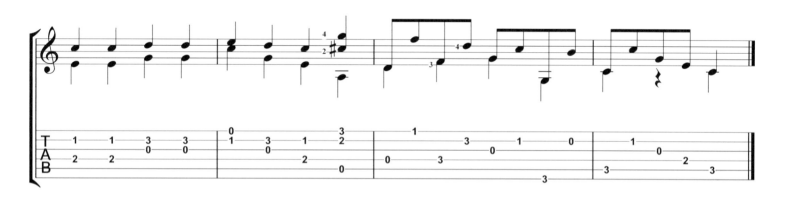

# Andantino

Joseph Kuffner

# Andante

Joseph Kuffner

# Anglaise
## Op. 121, No. 6

Ferdinando Carulli

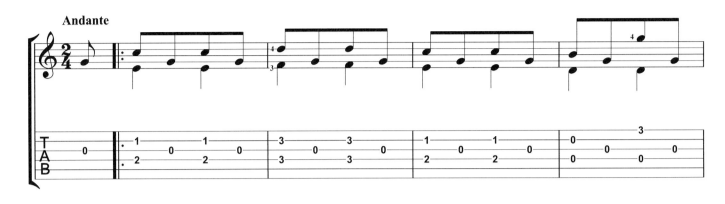

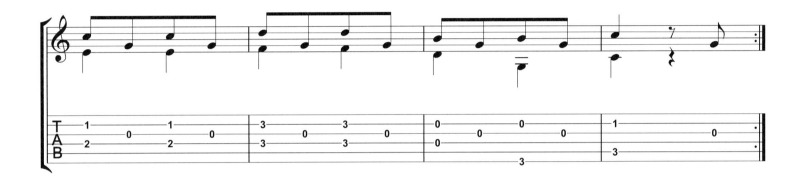

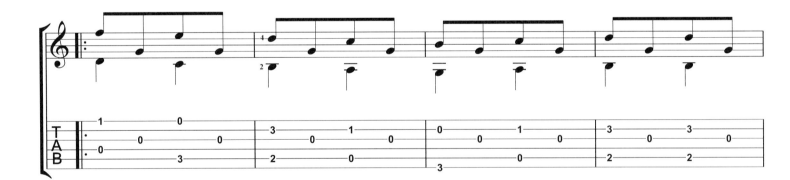

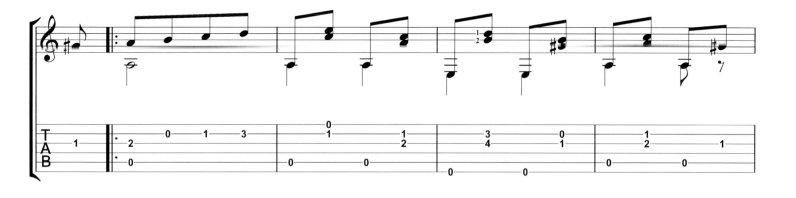

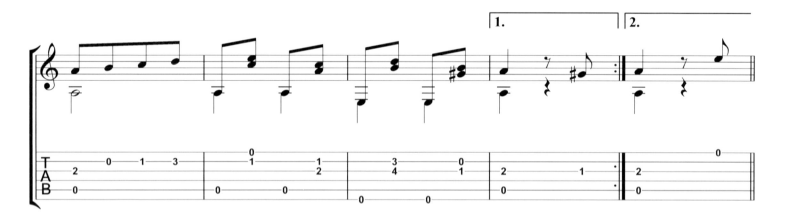

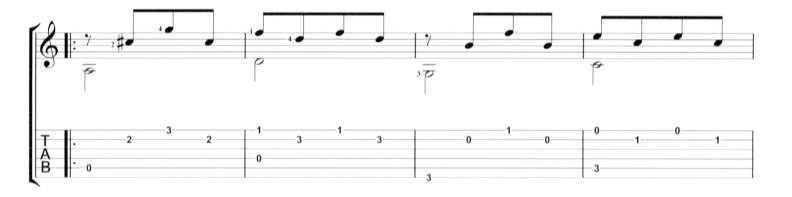

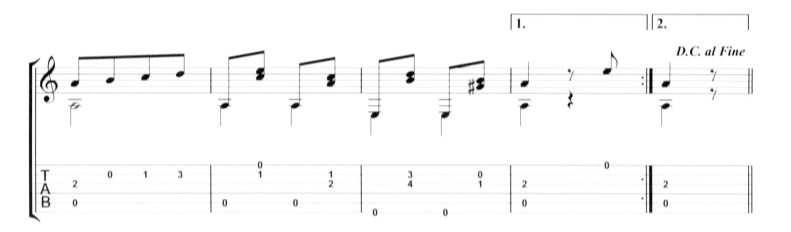

# Larghetto espressivo

Ferdinando Carulli

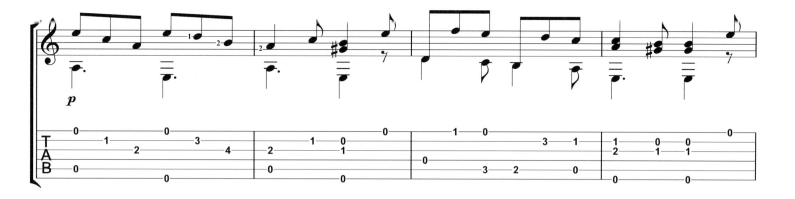

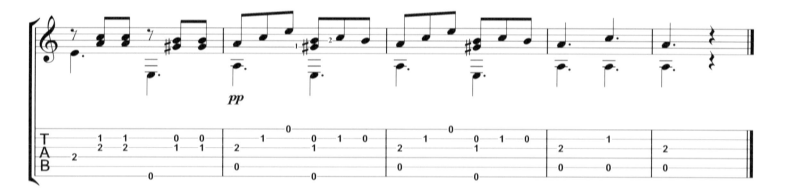

# Allegretto

Joseph Kuffner

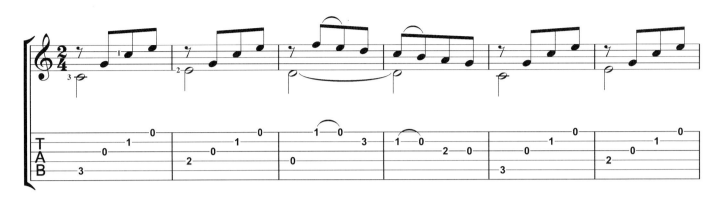

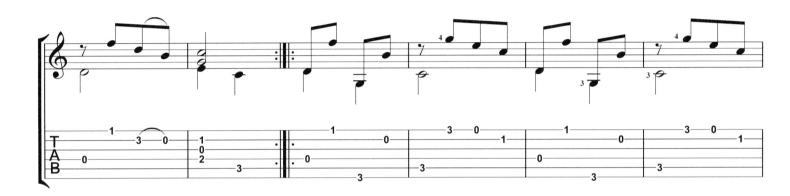

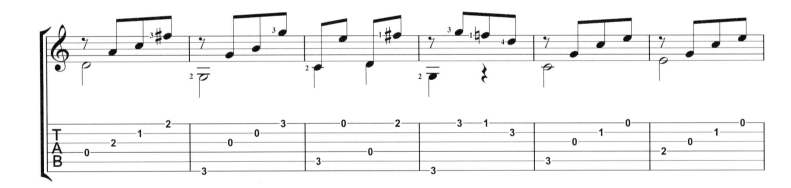

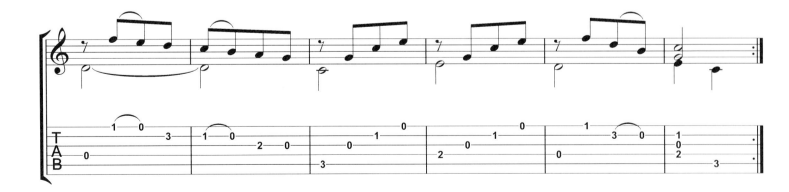

# Waltz

Joseph Kuffner

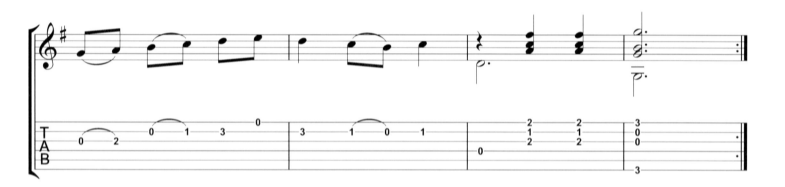

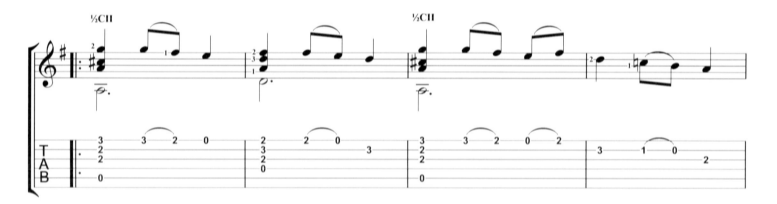

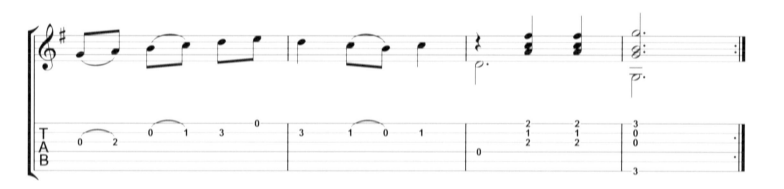

# Waltz

Matteo Carcassi (1792–1853)

# Enfantillage

Jacques Bosch (1825–1895)

# Andante

Joseph Kuffner

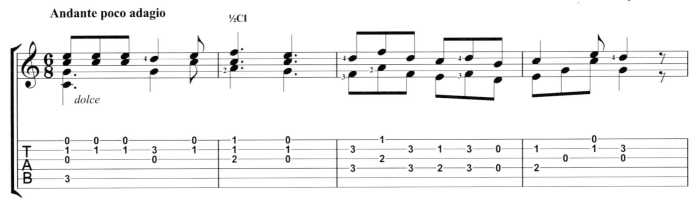

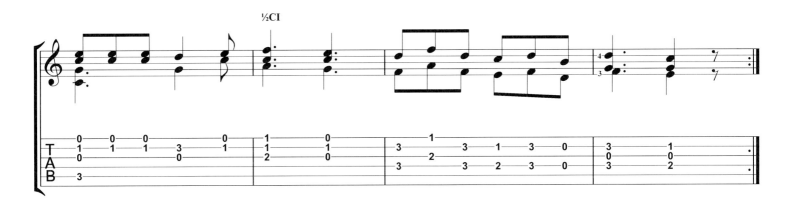

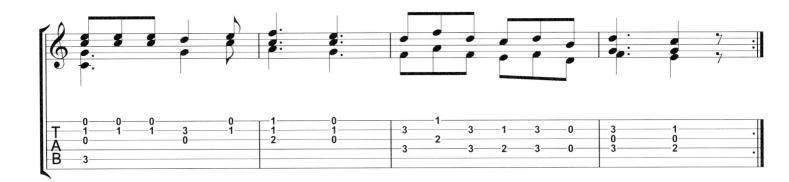

# Poco allegretto

Ferdinando Carulli

# Andante

Ferdinando Carulli

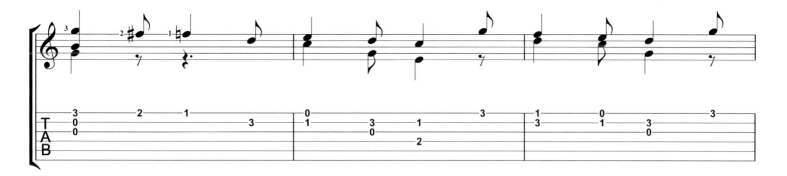

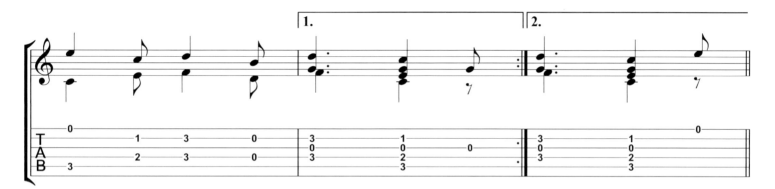

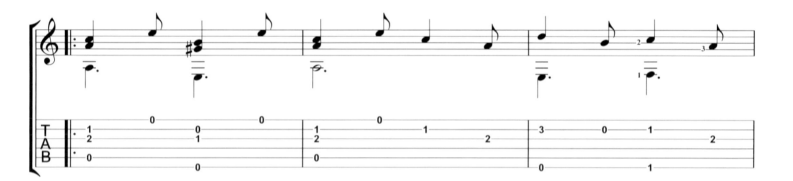

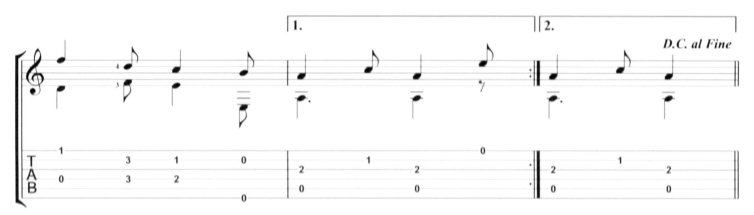

# Branle de Bourgogne

Adrian Le Roy (1520–1598)

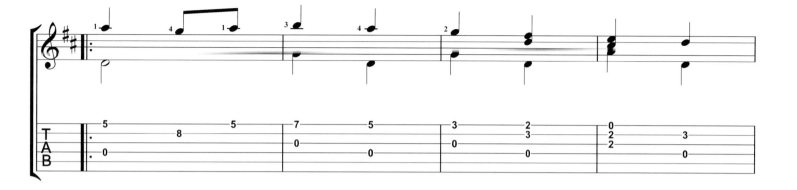

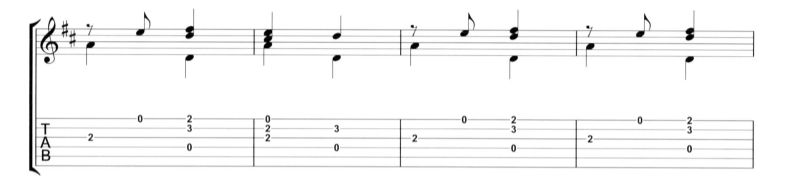

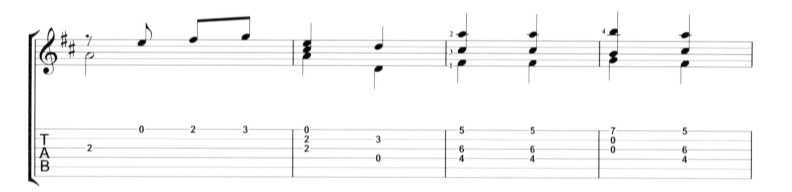

# Canario

Carlo Calvi (ca. 1610–ca. 1646)

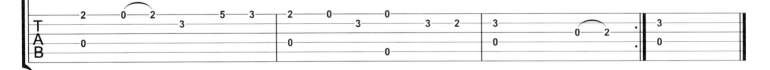

# Tordiglione

Carlo Calvi

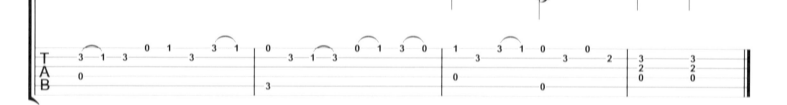

# Allegretto

Francesco Batioli (1830–1861)

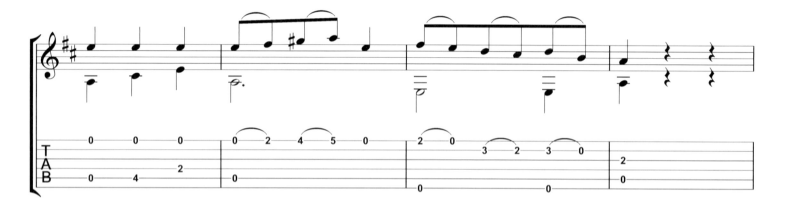

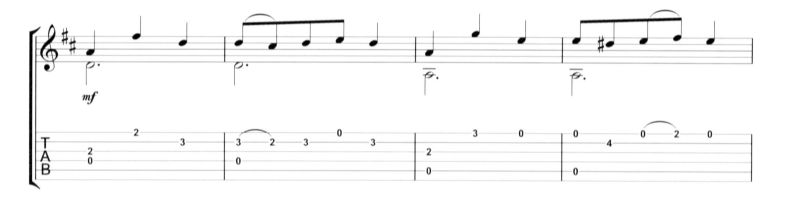

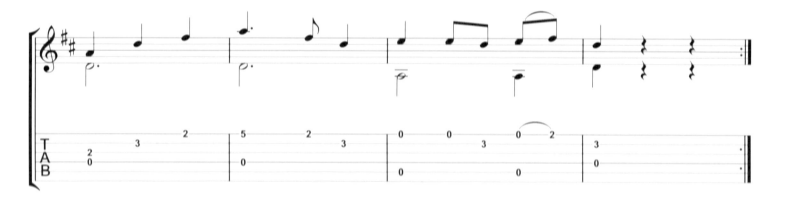

# Dance

Joan Ambrosio Dalza (fl. 1508)

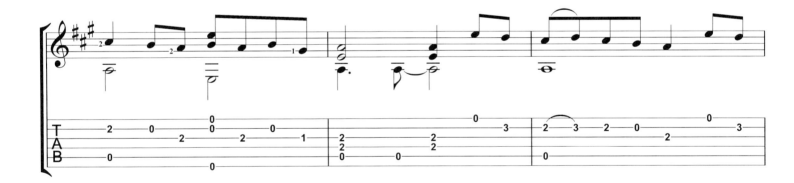

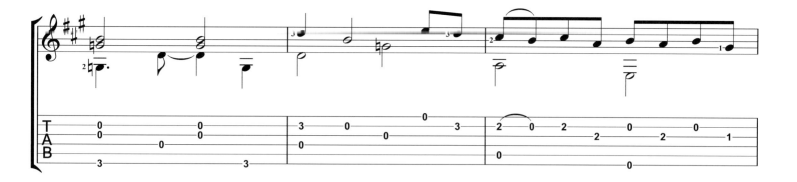

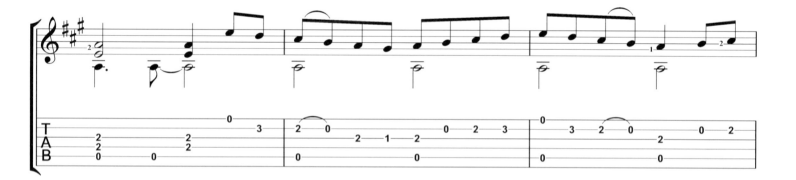

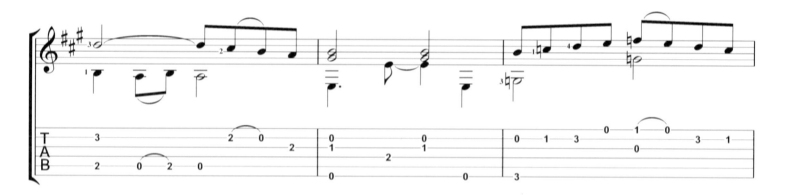

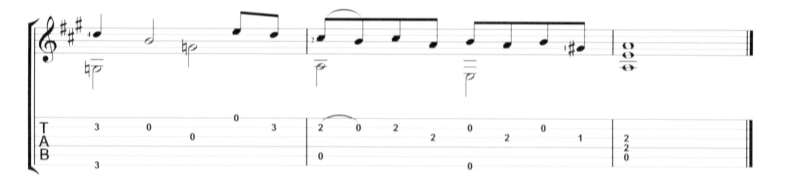

# Allegro

Mauro Giuliani (1781–1829)

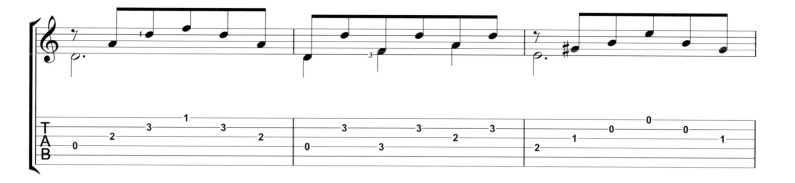

# Moderato

Matteo Carcassi

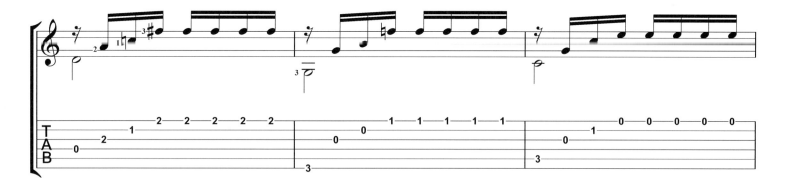

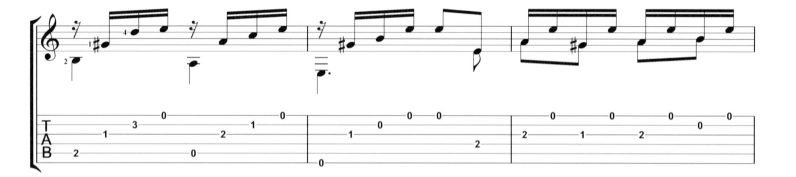

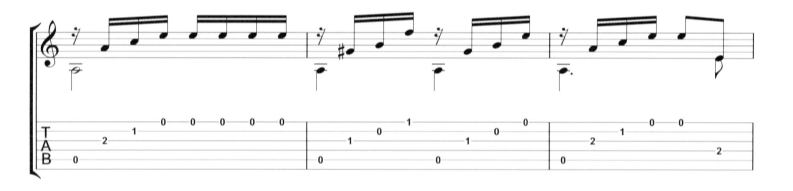

# Das klinget so herrlich
# ("It rings out so joyful"
# from *The Magic Flute*)

Francesco Batioli/W. A. Mozart

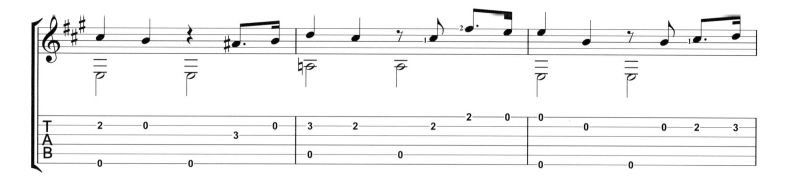

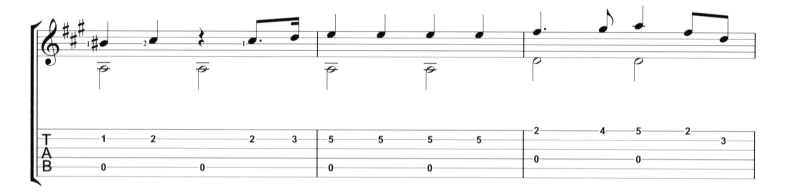

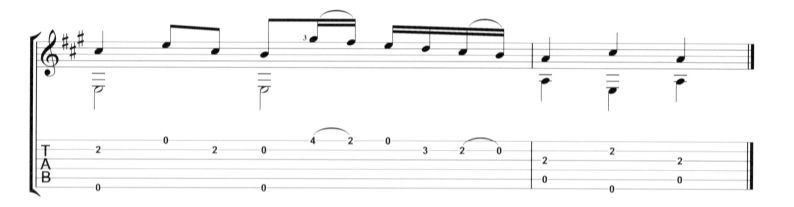

# Aria

Giuseppe Antonio Brescianello (ca. 1690–1758)

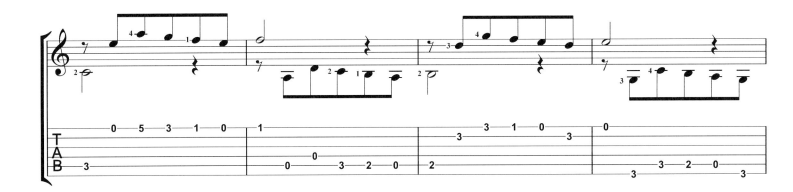

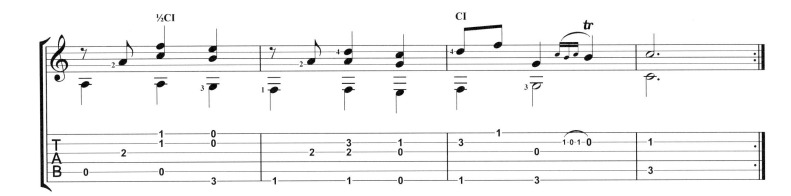

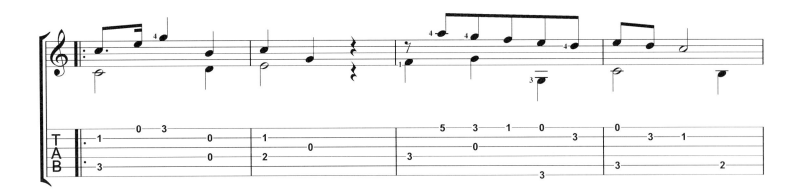

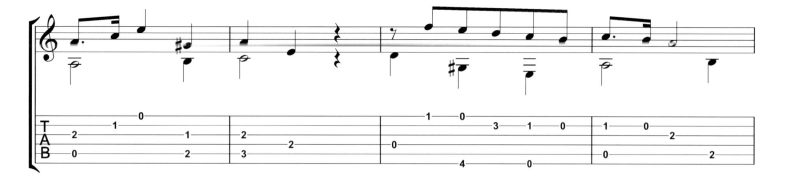

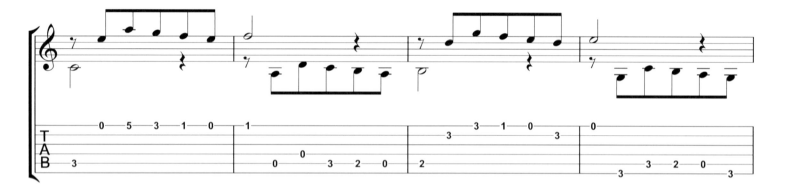

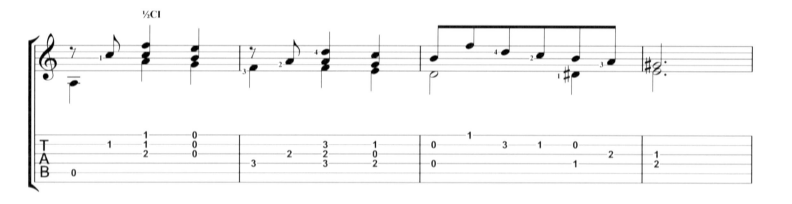

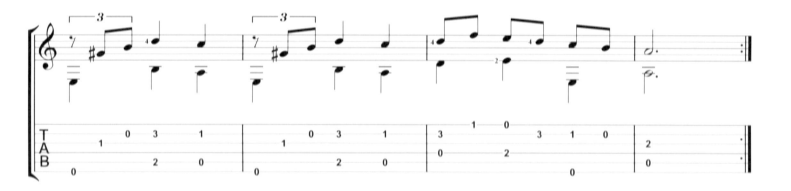

# Menuett

Giuseppe Antonio Brescianello

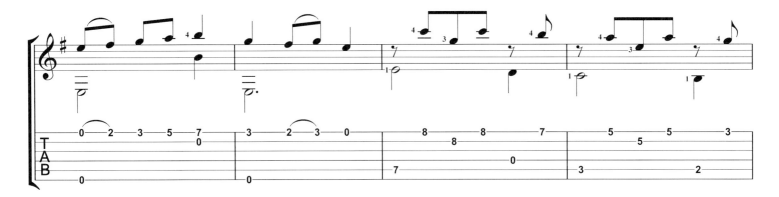

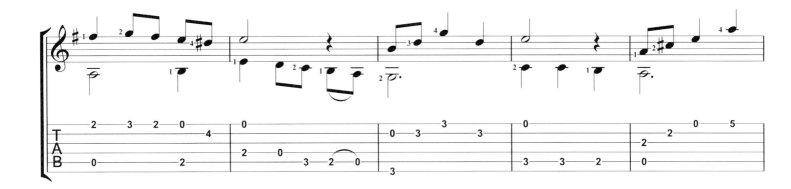

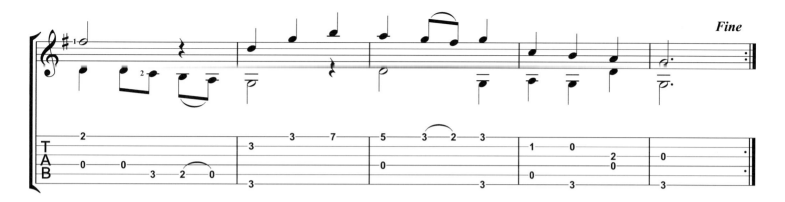

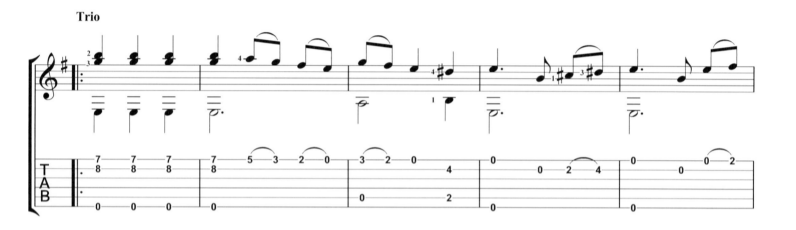

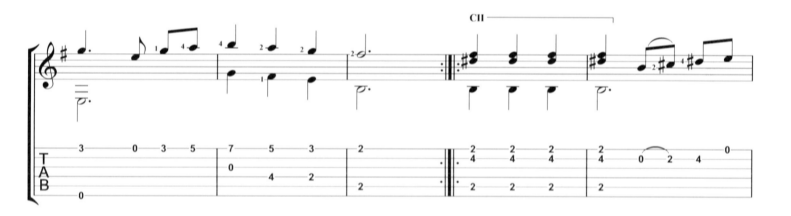

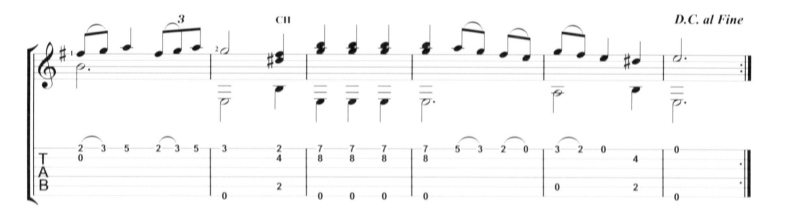

# Guagirana No. 1

Jacques Bosch

**Allegro moderato**

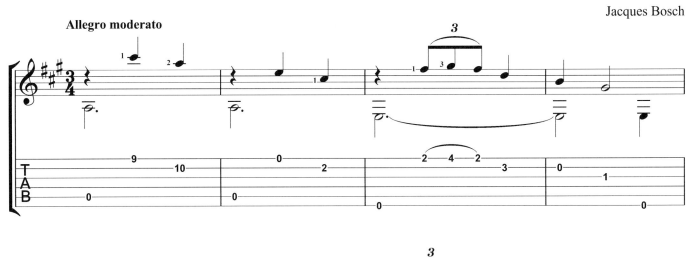

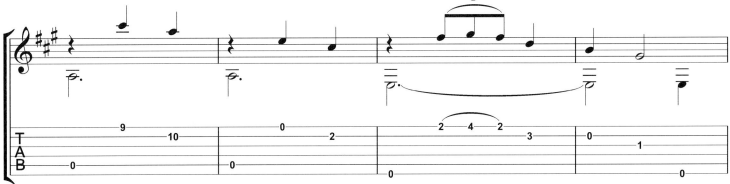

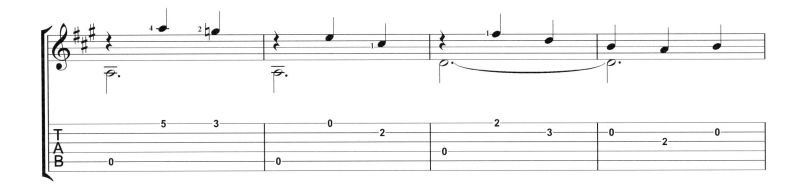

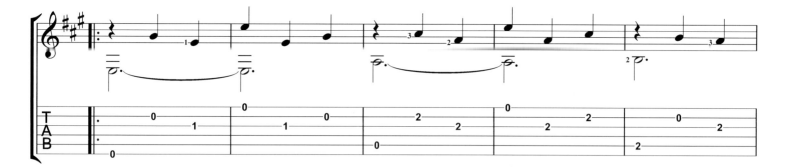

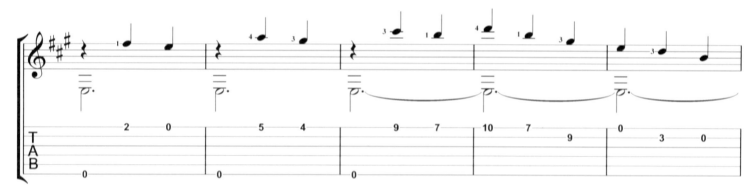

*D.C. al Coda*     Φ *Coda*

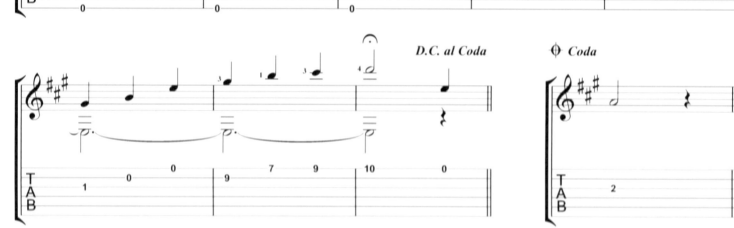

# Guagirana No. 2

Jacques Bosch

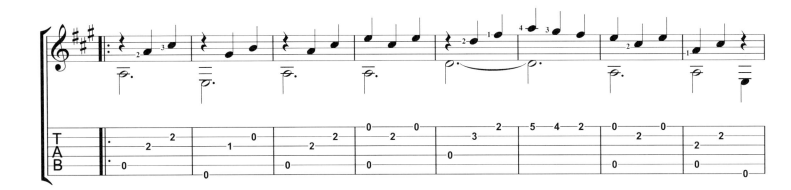

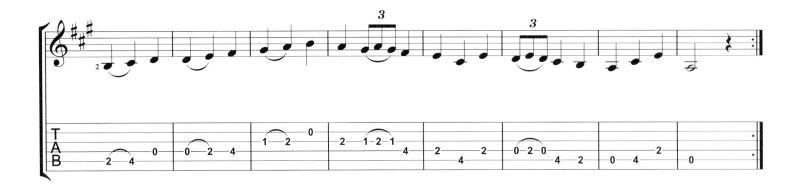

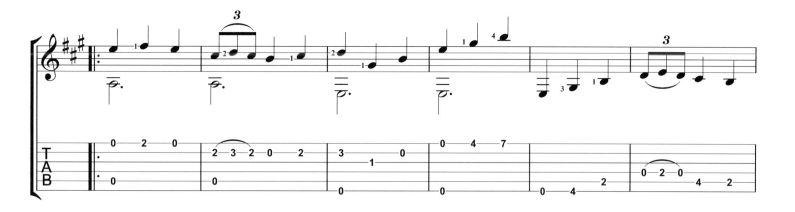

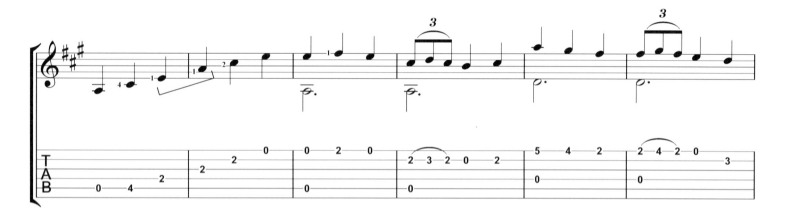

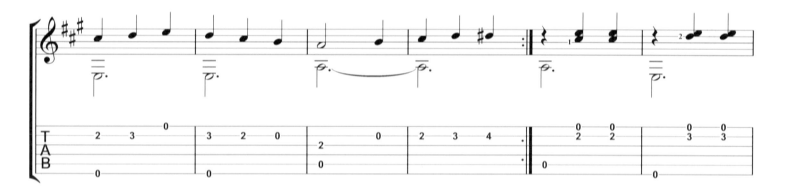

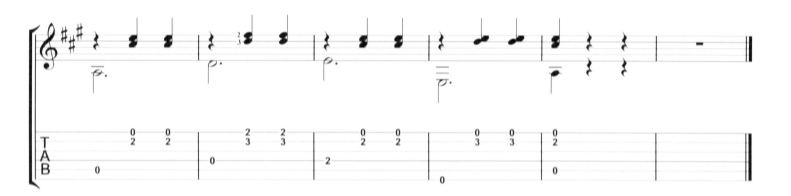

# Andantino

Johann Mertz (1806–1856)

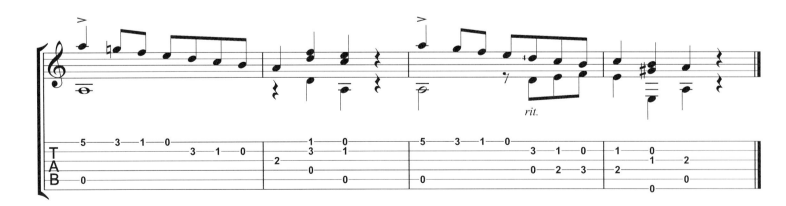

# Andantino

Johann Mertz

# Allegretto

Johann Mertz

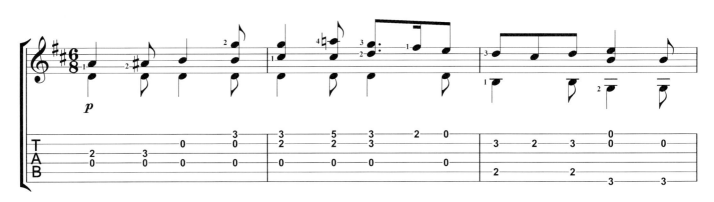

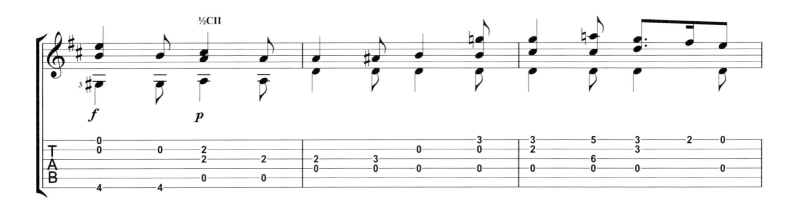

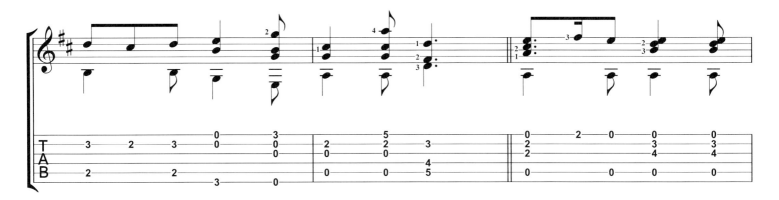

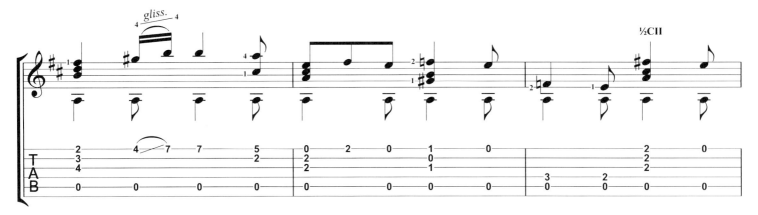

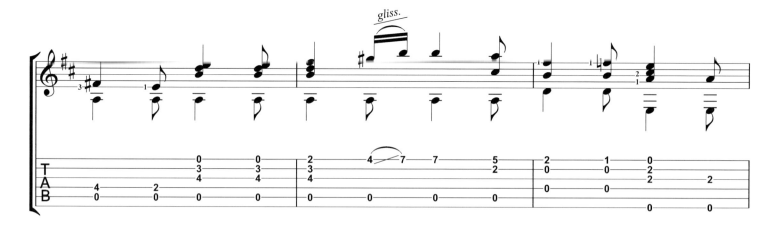

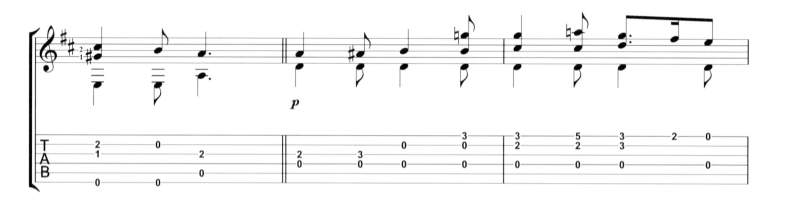

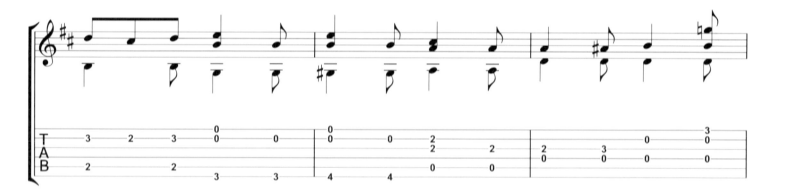

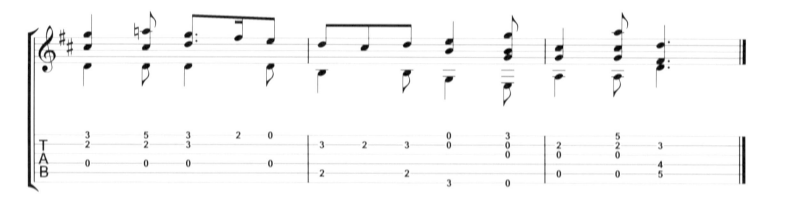

# Andante

Johann Mertz

# Andante grazioso

Ferdinando Carulli

# Romance

Johann Mertz

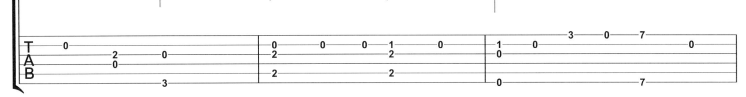

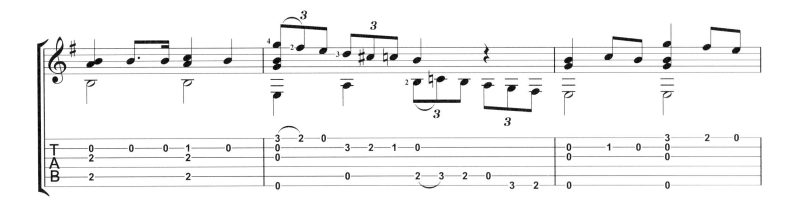

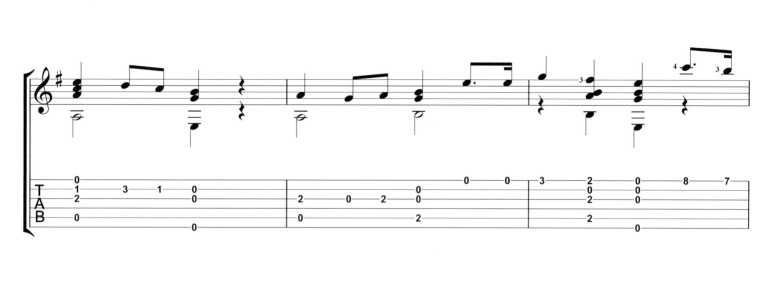

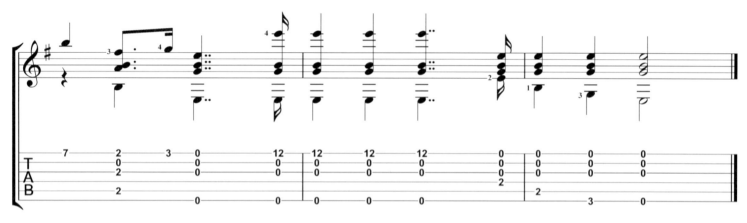

# Moderato

Johann Mertz

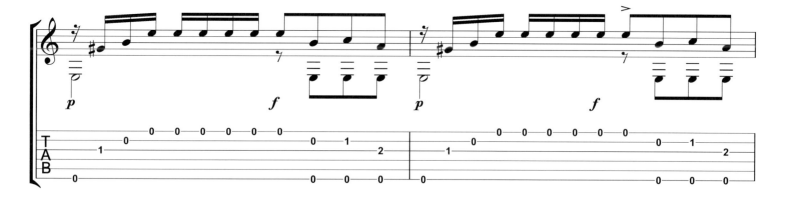

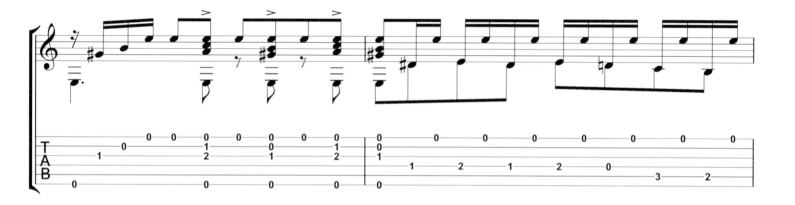

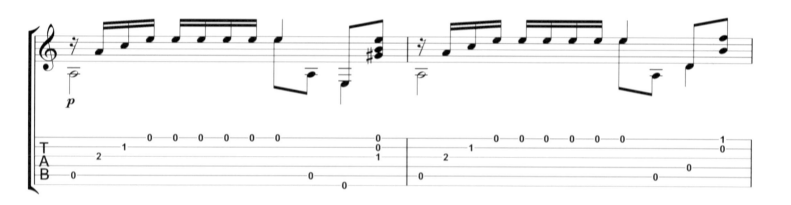

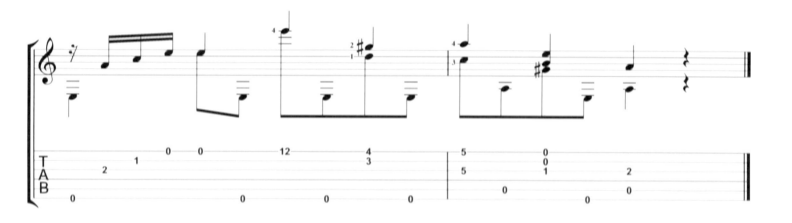

# Andante

Johann Mertz

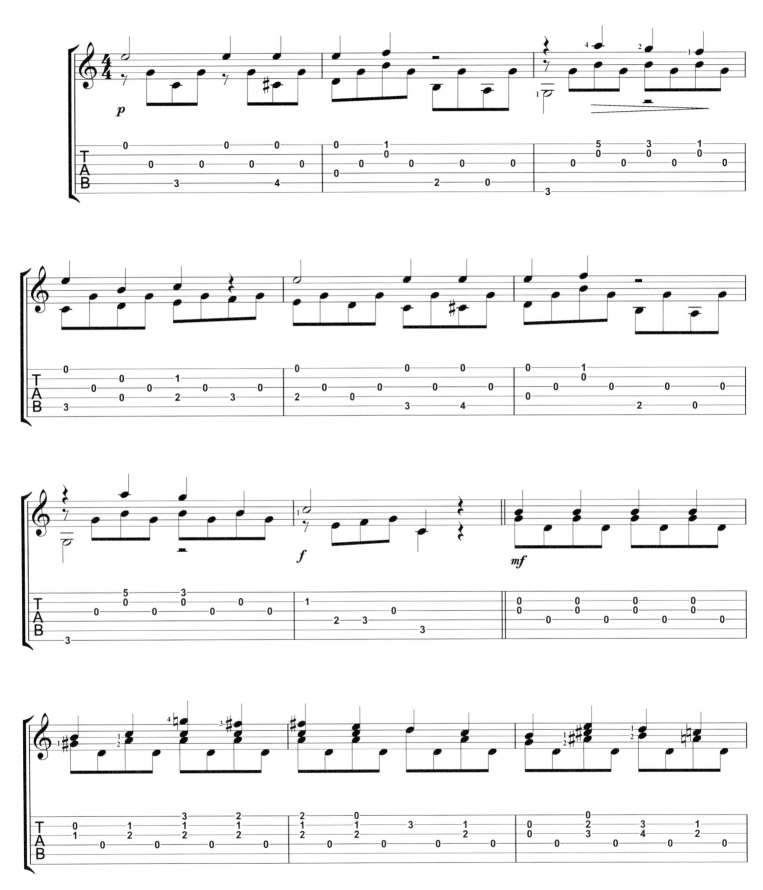

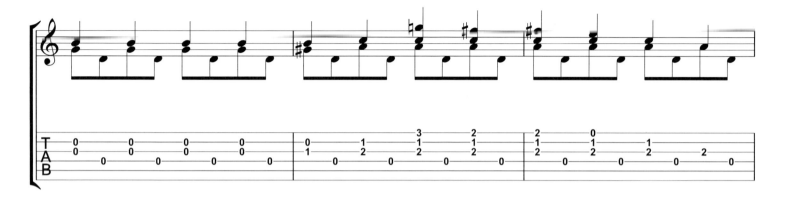

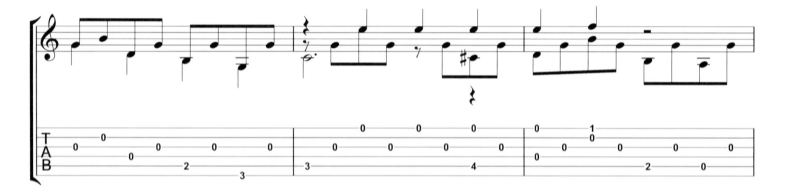

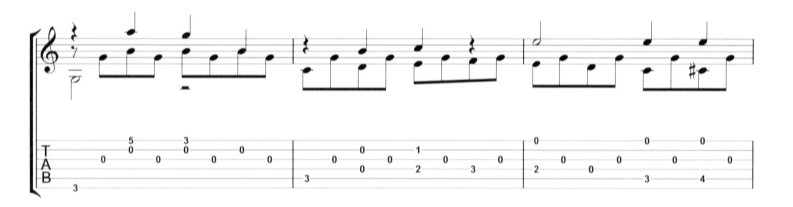

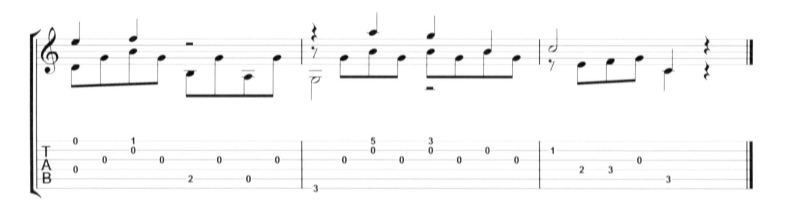

# Etude No. 2

Mauro Giuliani

**Allegretto**

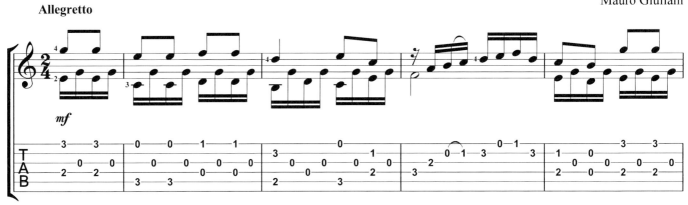

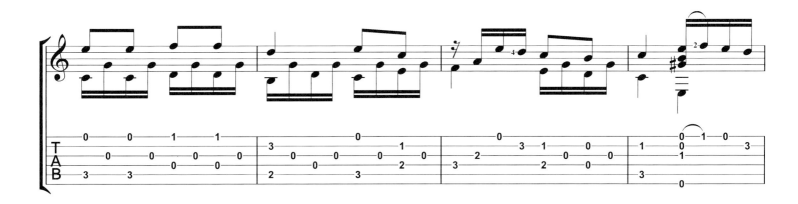

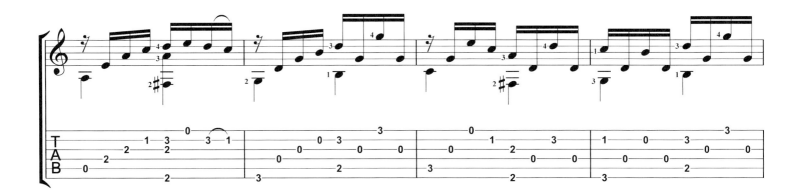

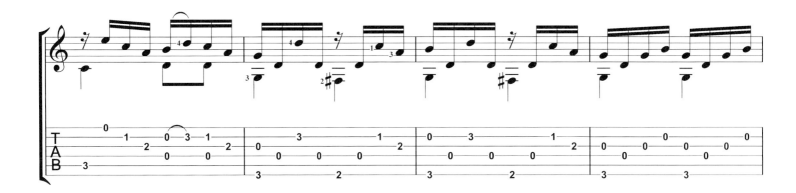

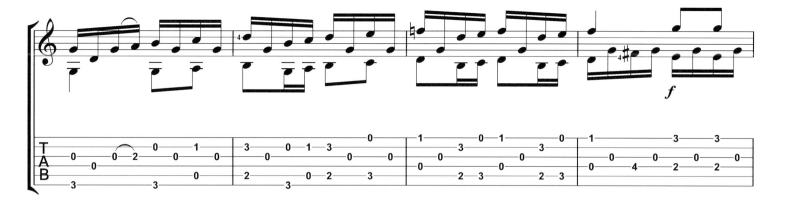

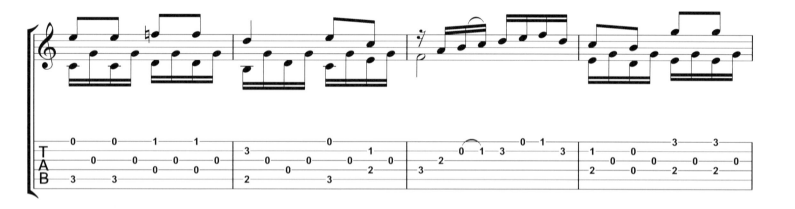

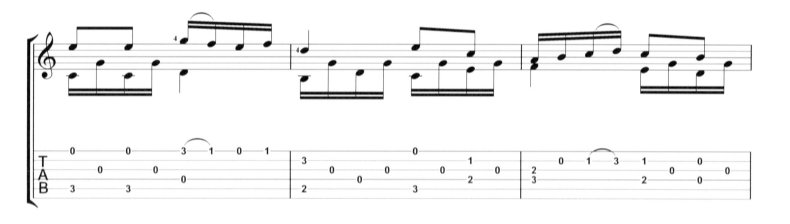

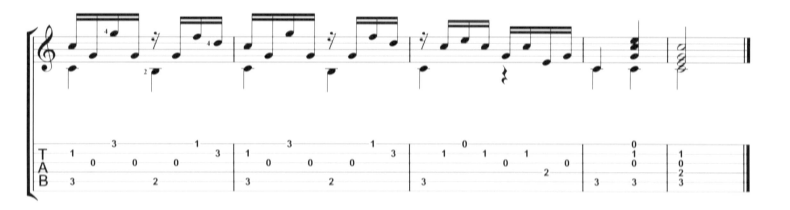

# Study No. 4

Fernando Sor (1778–1839)

**Moderato**

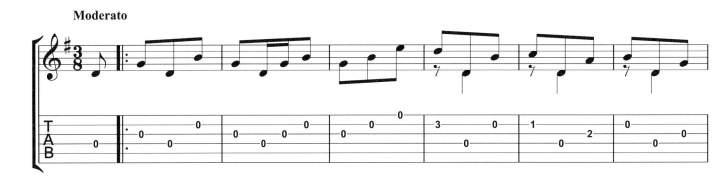

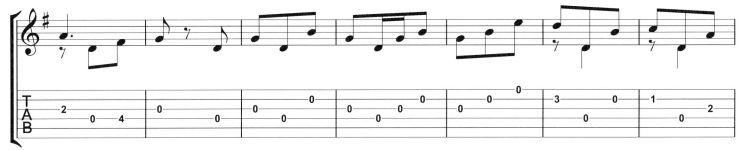

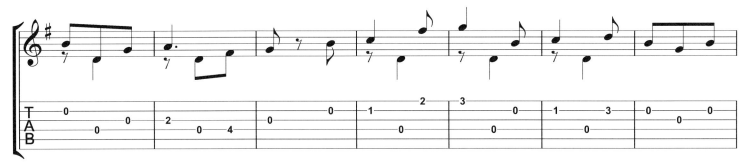

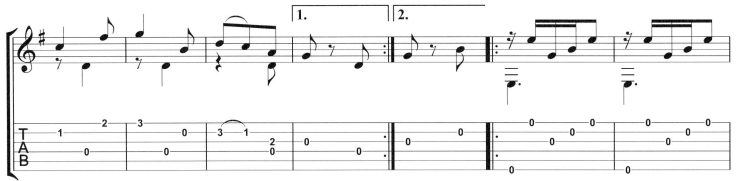

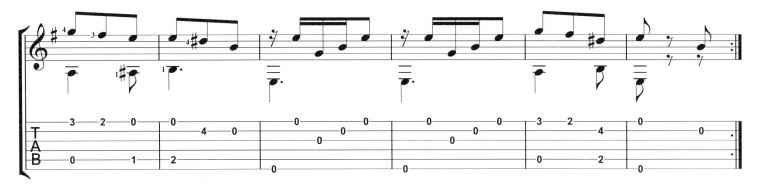

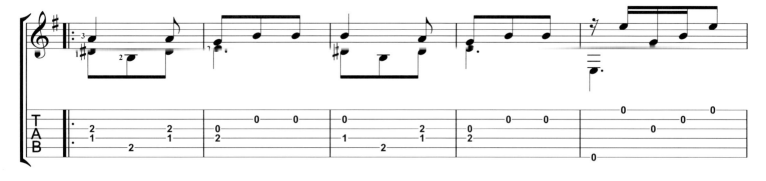

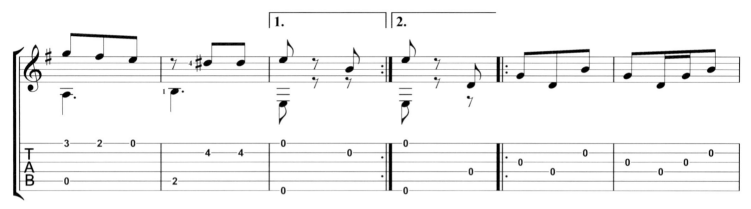

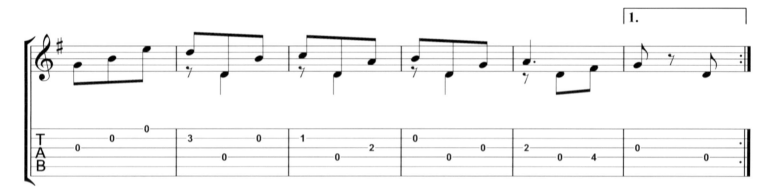

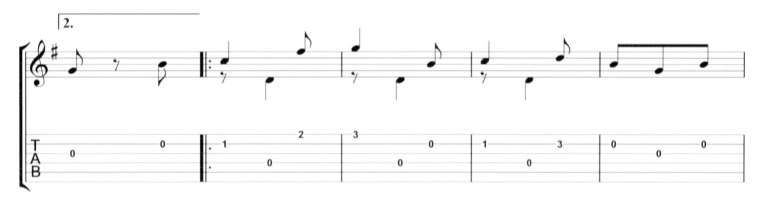

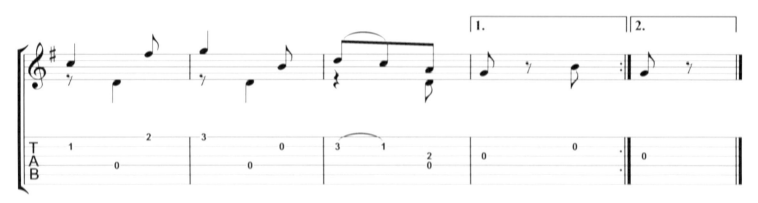

# Valse

José Ferrer (1835–1916)

**Moderately**

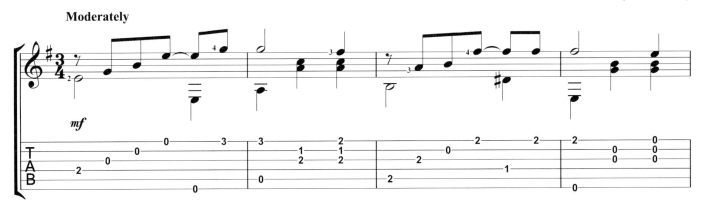

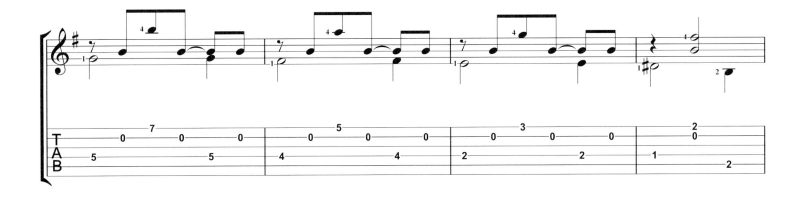

*Fine*

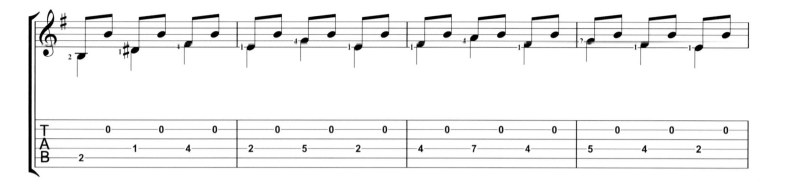

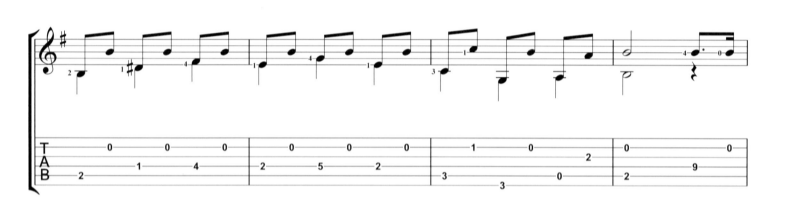

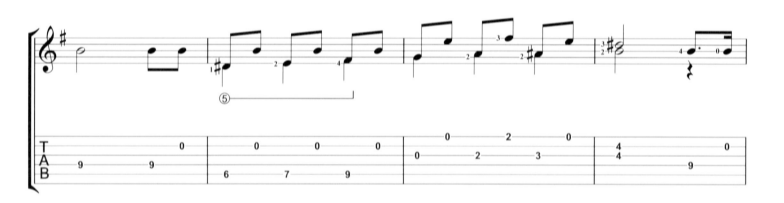

*D.C. al Fine*

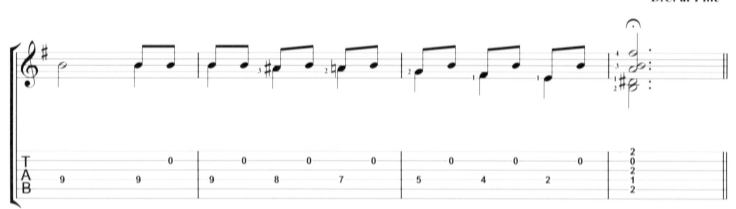

# Romance

Francesco Molino (1775–1847)

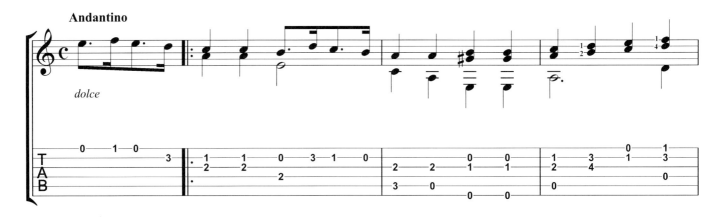

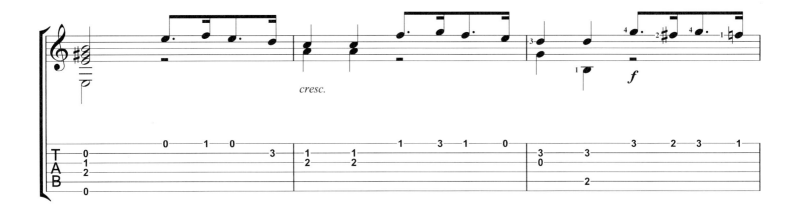

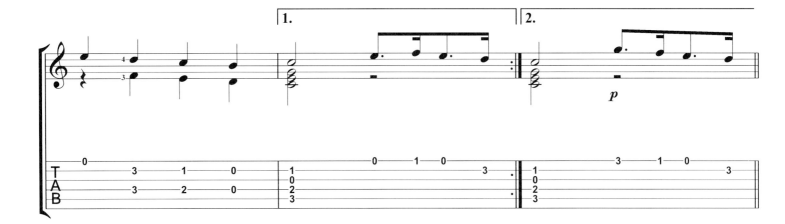

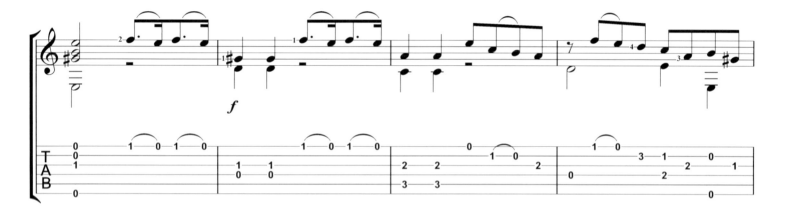

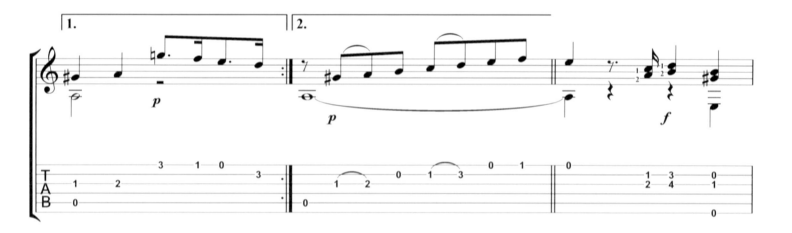

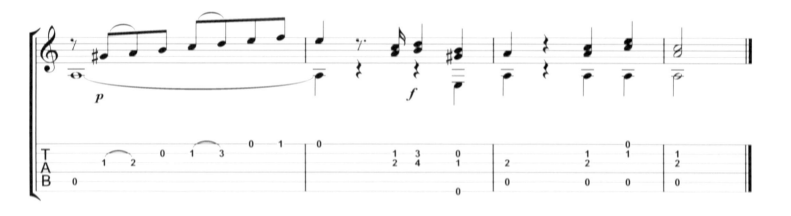

# El Vito

Anonymous
(Spanish Folk Song)

**Allegretto**

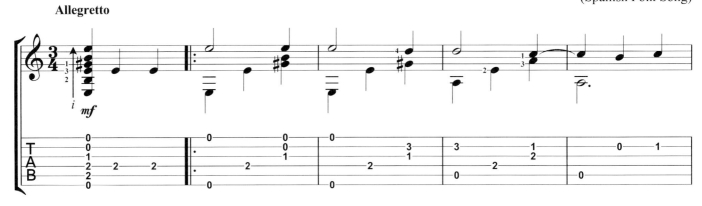

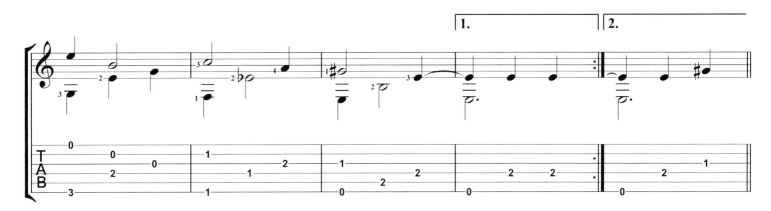

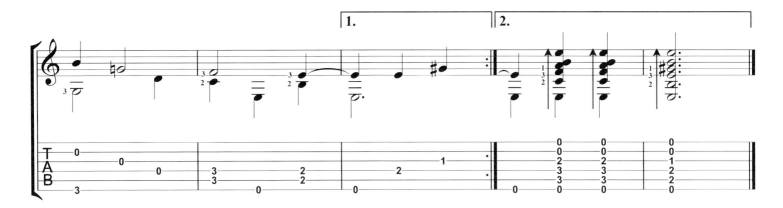

# Lamento

Jacques Bosch

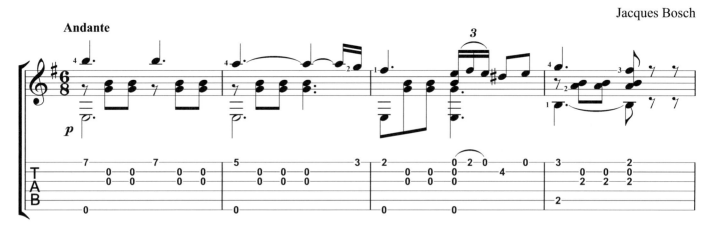

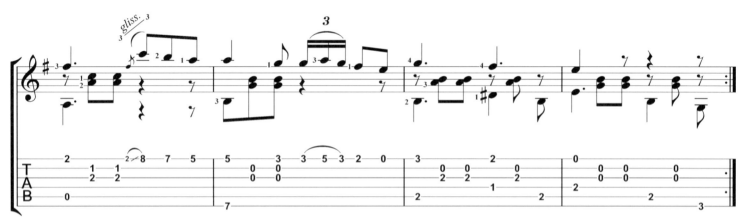

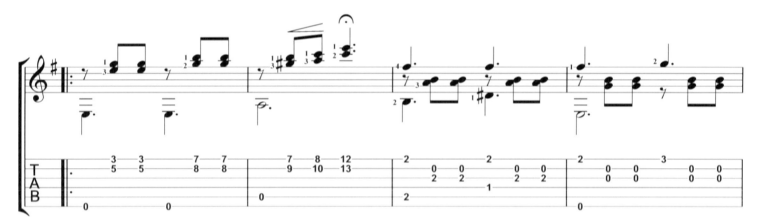

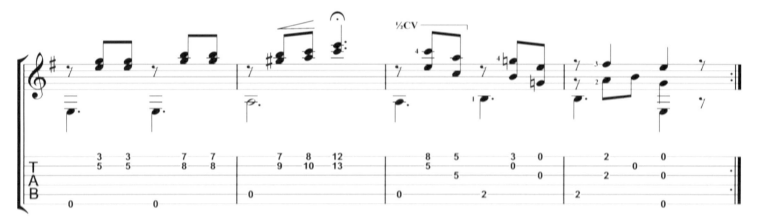

# El Noi de la Mare

Anonymous
(Spanish Folk Song)

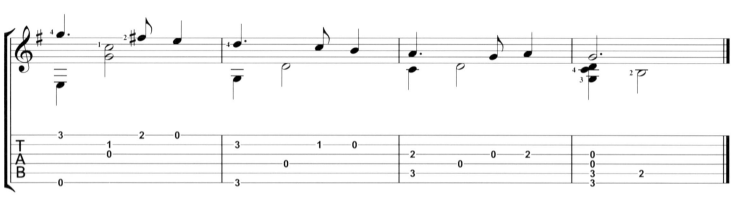

# Spanish Romance

Anonymous
(Spanish Folk Song)

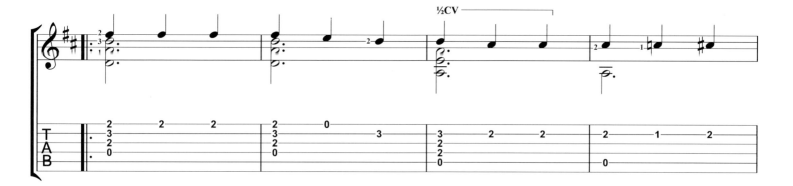

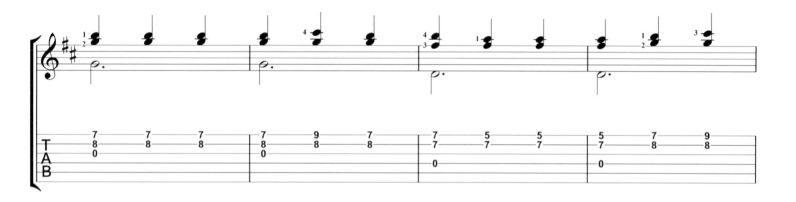

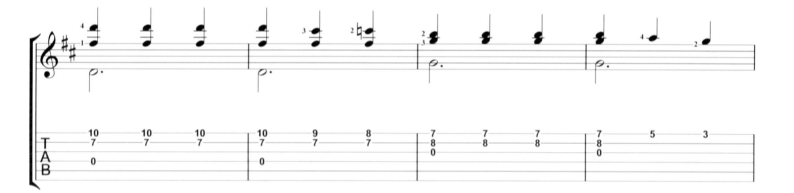

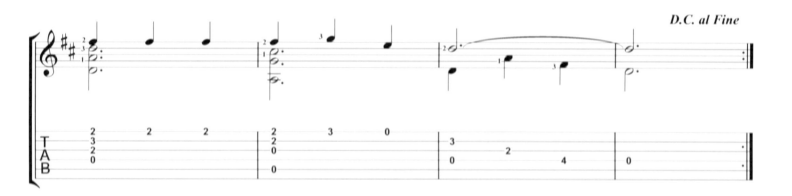

# Anitra's Dance

Edvard Grieg (1843–1907)

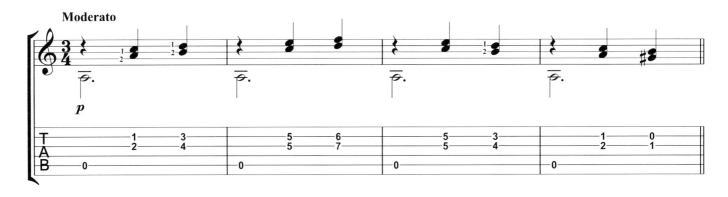

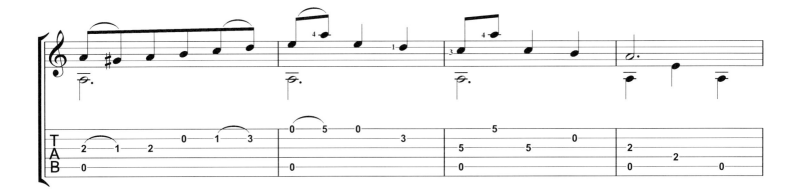

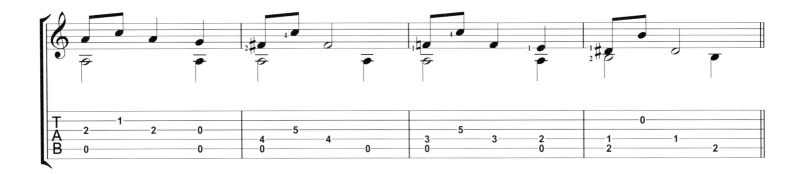

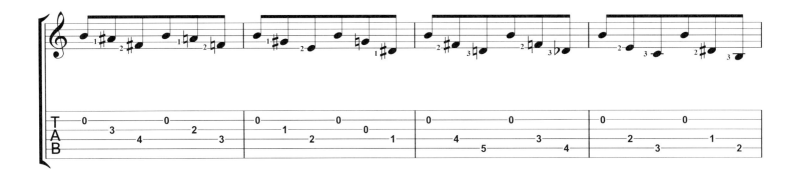

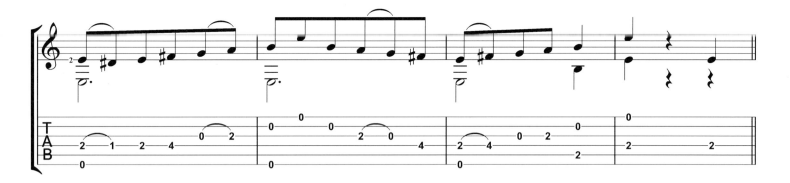

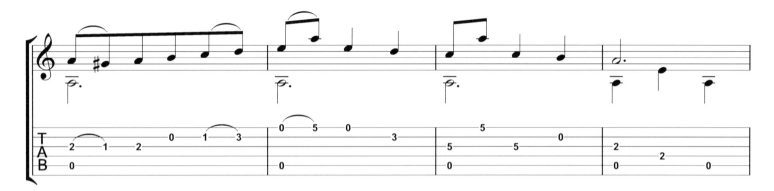

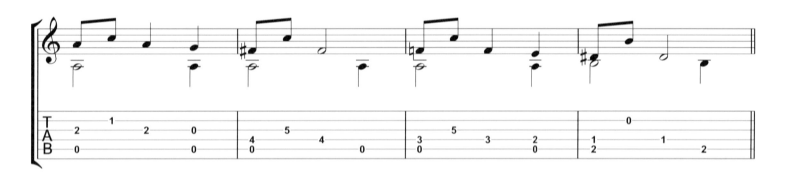

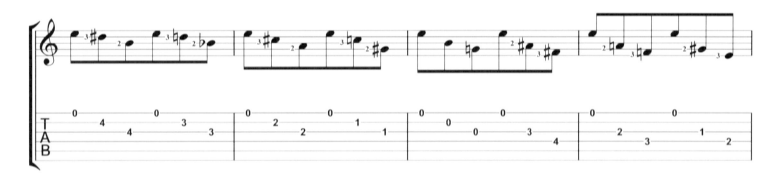

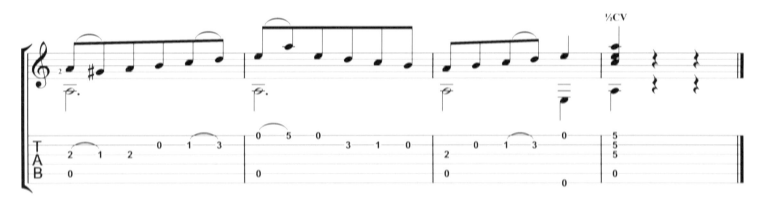

# Sonatina No. 1

**Allegro**

Niccolo Paganini (1782–1840)

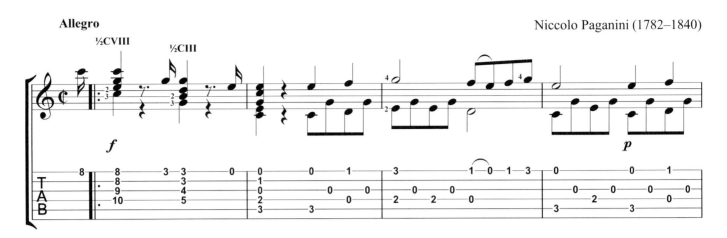

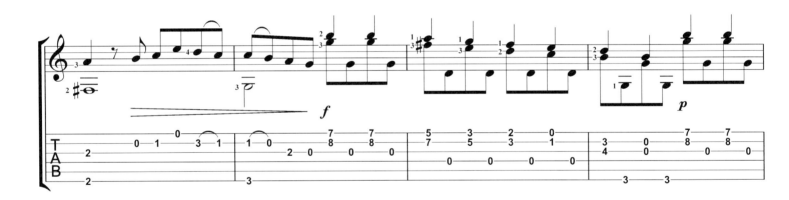

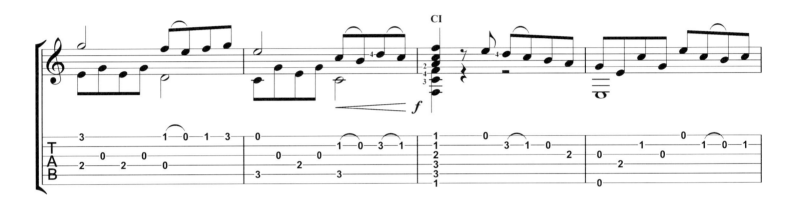

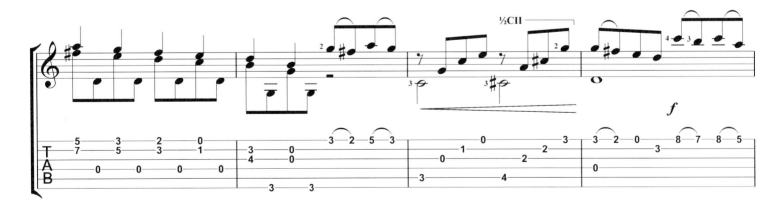

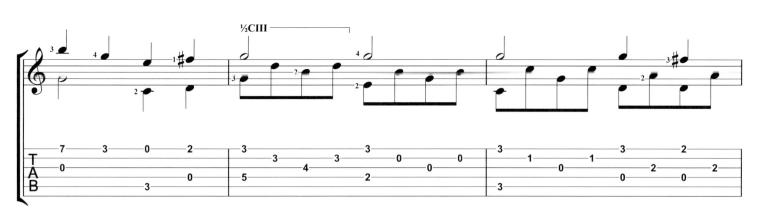

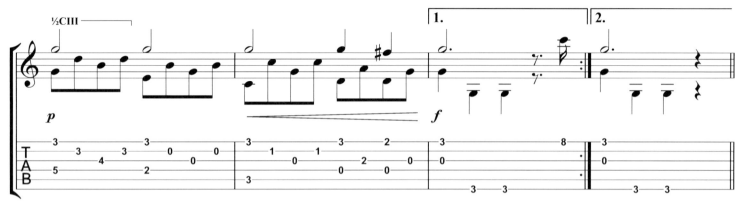

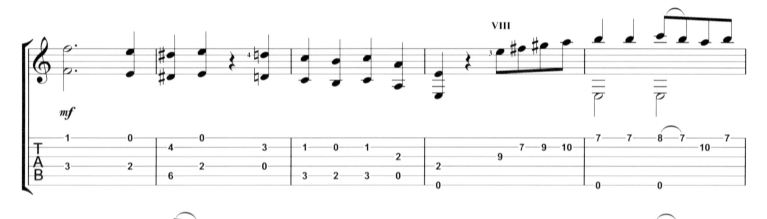

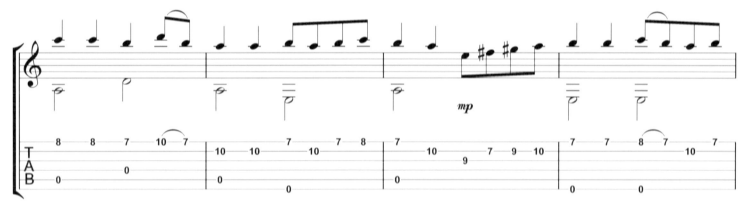

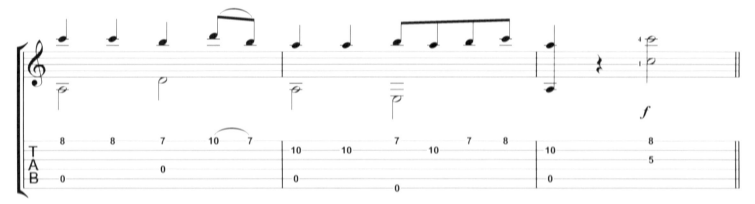

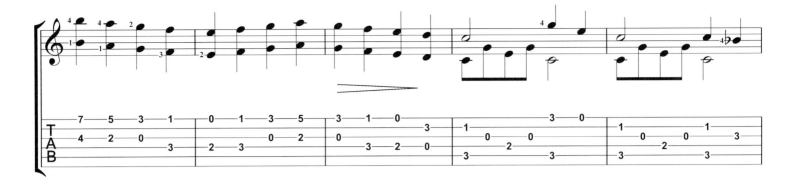

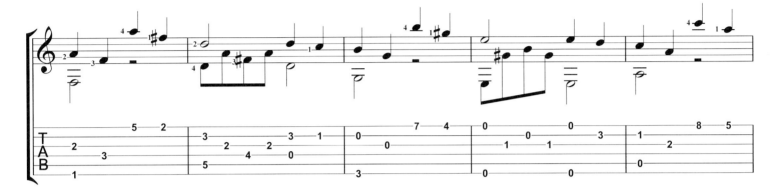

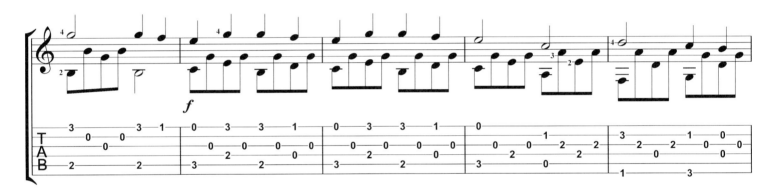

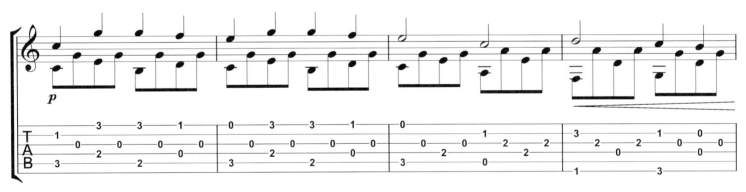

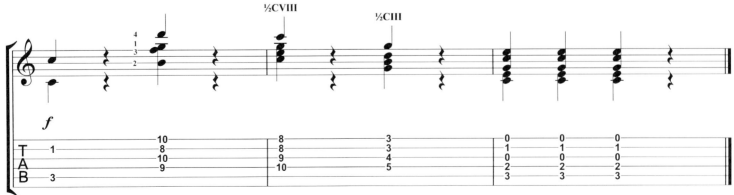

# Malagueña

Anonymous/traditional
(Spanish Dance)

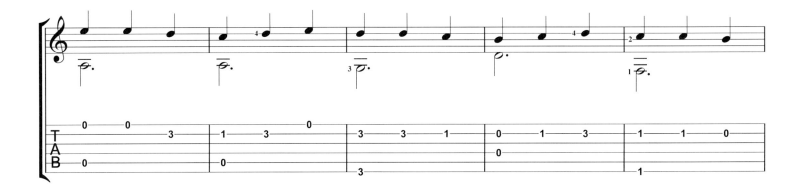

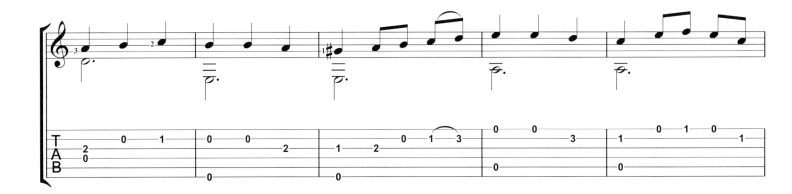

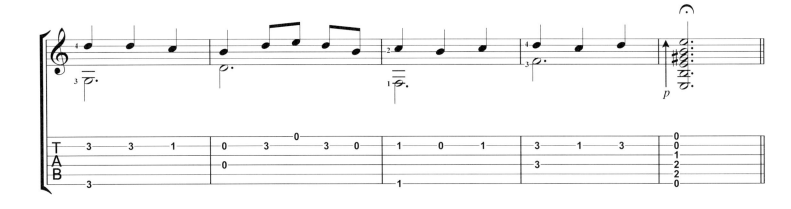

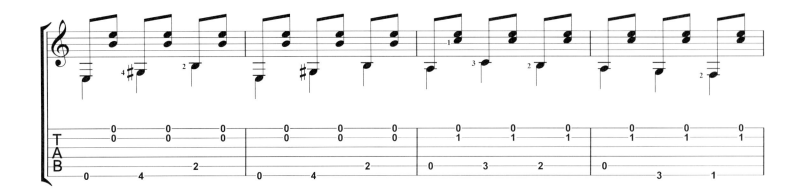

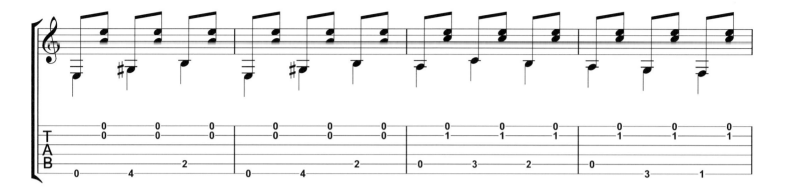

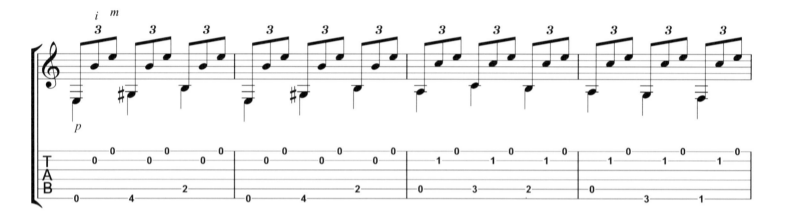

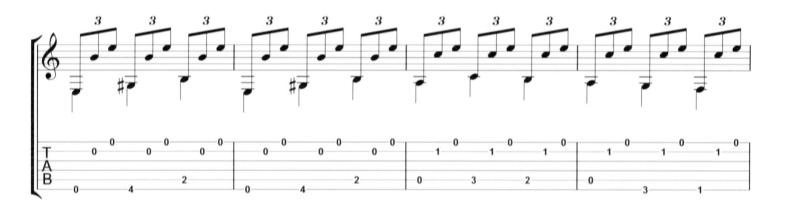

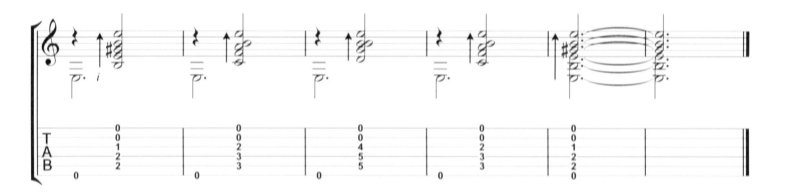

# Andantino

Niccolo Paganini

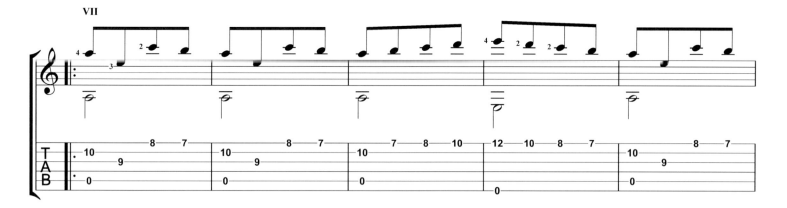

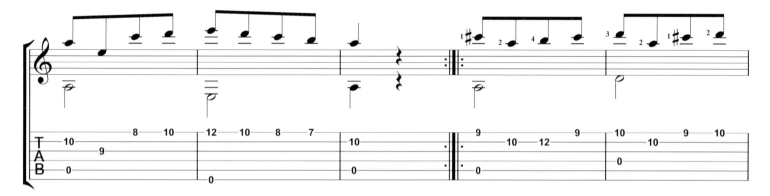

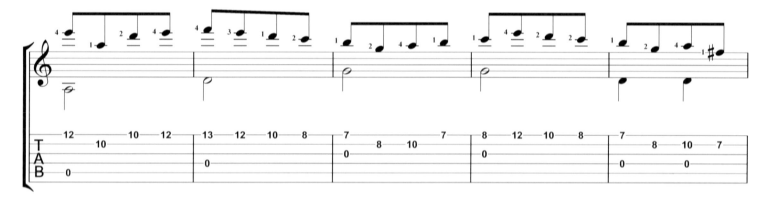

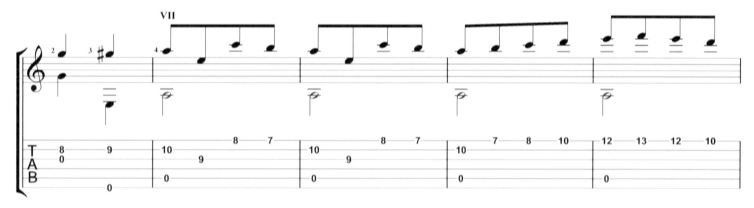

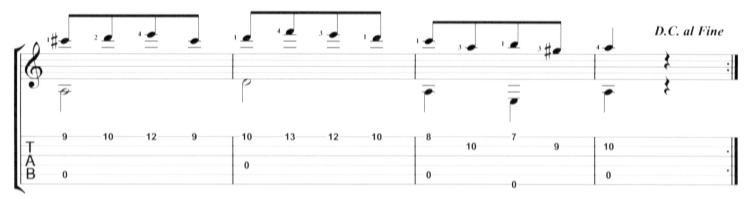

*D.C. al Fine*

# Perligordino

Niccolo Paganini

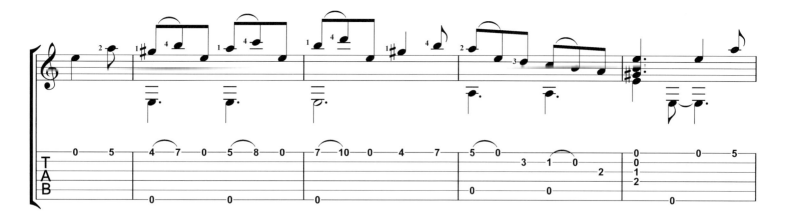

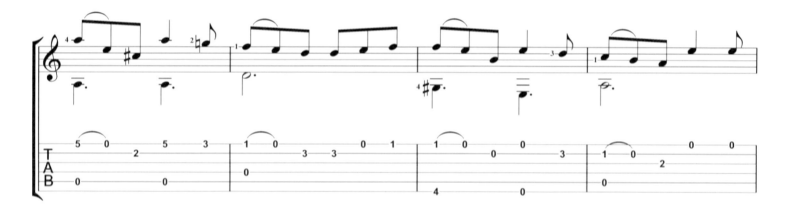

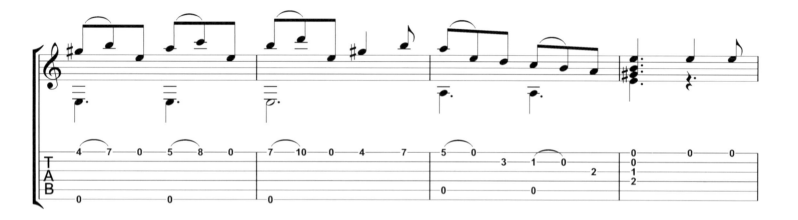

*D.C. al Fine*

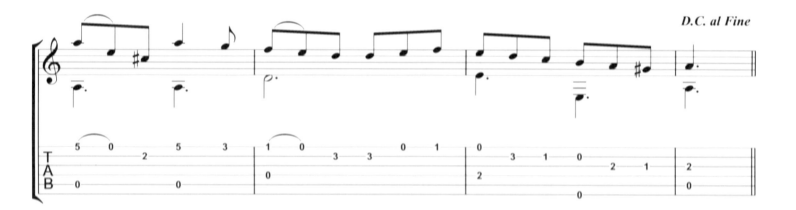

# Le Streghe

Niccolo Paganini

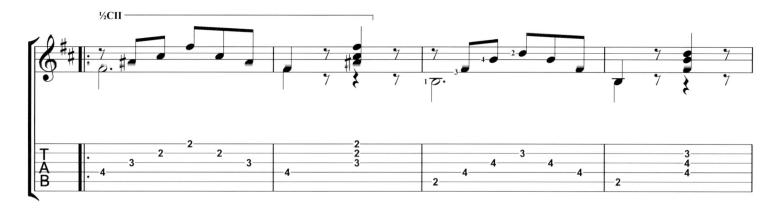

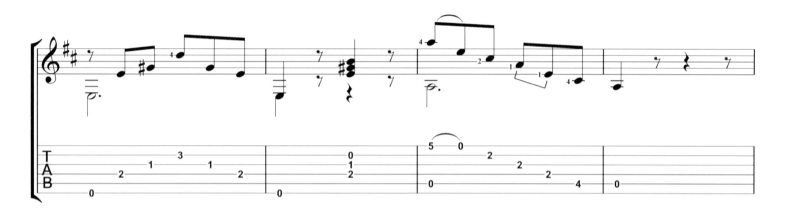

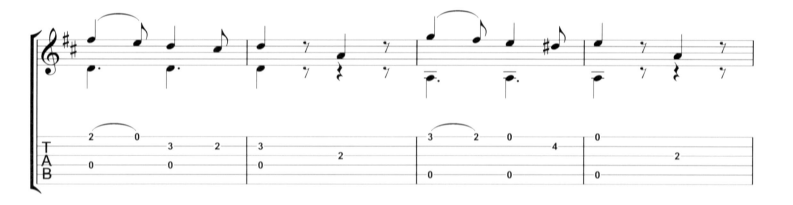

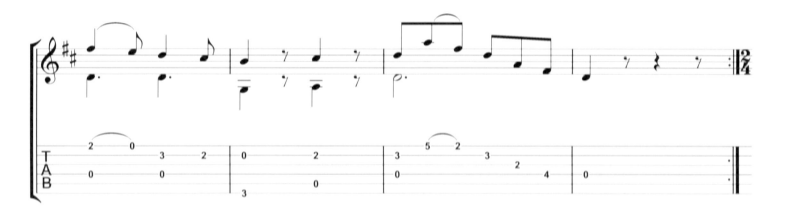

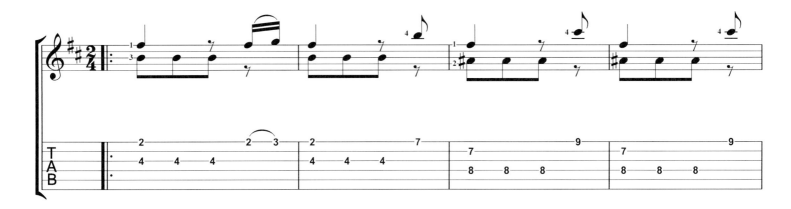

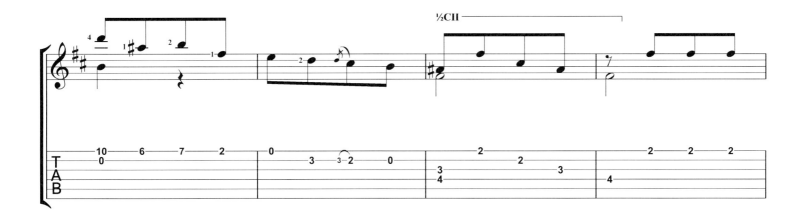

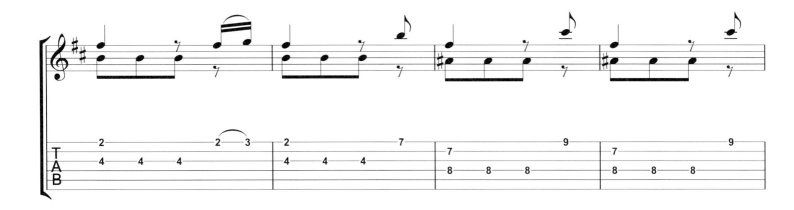

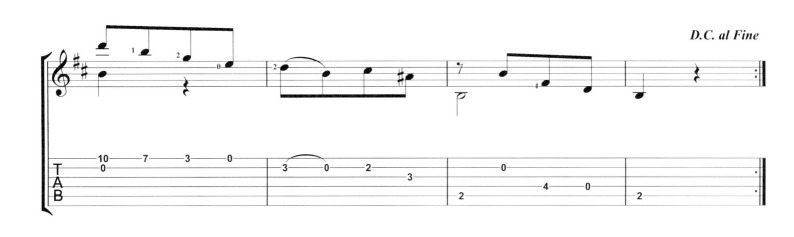

# L' Étudiant de Salamanque

José Ferrer

**Moderate tango**

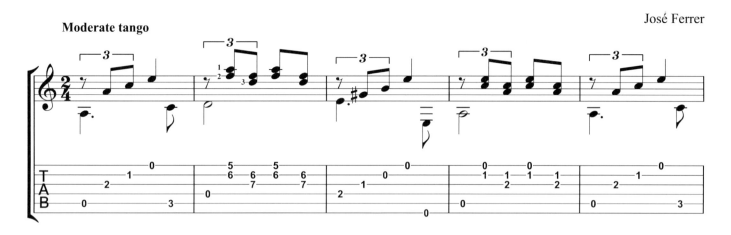

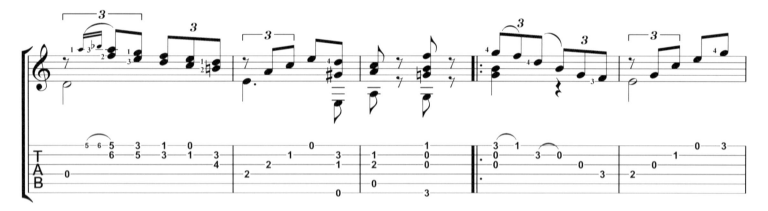

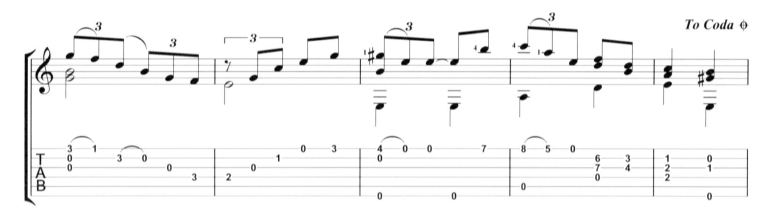

*To Coda* ⊕

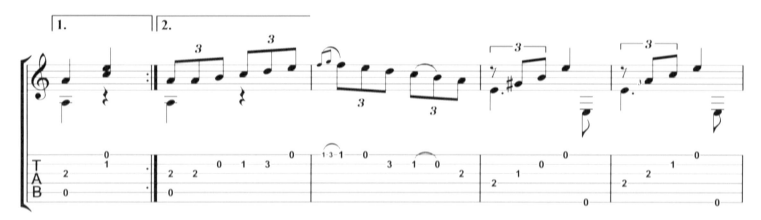

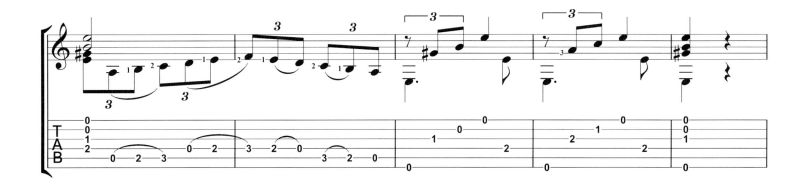

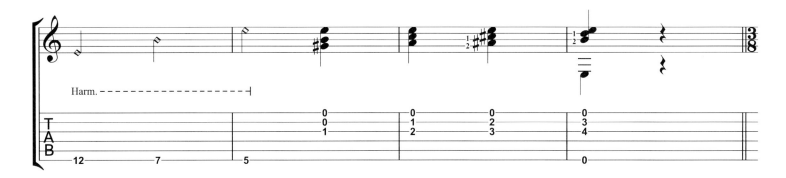

**Tempo di valse**

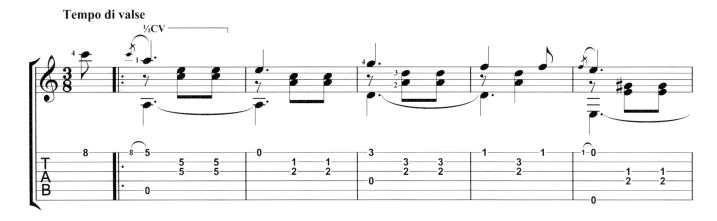

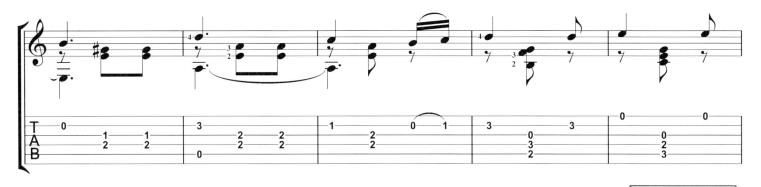

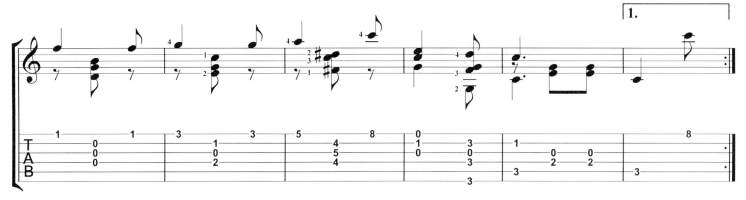

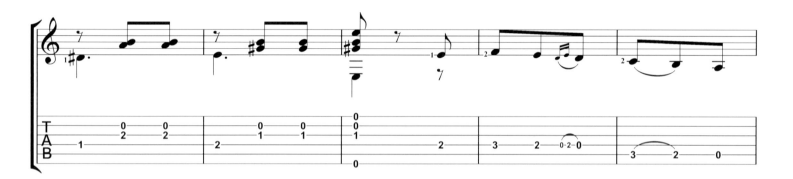

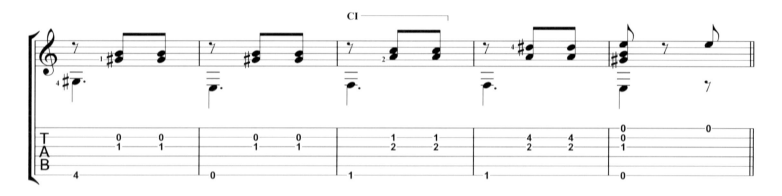

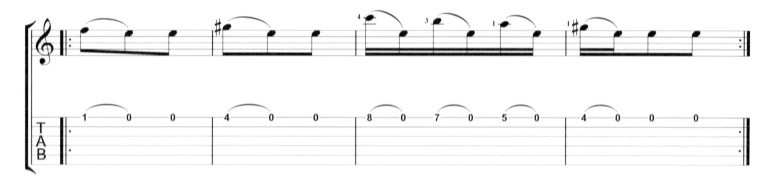

*D.C. al Coda*   **Φ** *Coda*

# Index of Composers